ANGELS OF THE LYRE

ANGELS OF THE LYRE

A GAY POETRY ANTHOLOGY

Edited by Winston Leyland

Panjandrum Press · Gay Sunshine Press
San Francisco 1975

Robert Duncan's "The Torso Passages 18" from *Bending the Bow*, copyright ©
1968 by Robert Duncan. Reprinted by permission of New Directions Publishing
Corp. "This Place Rumord to Have Been Sodom" from *The Opening of the Field*,
copyright © 1960 by Robert Duncan. Reprinted by permission of New Directions
Publishing Corp.

Allen Ginsberg's "On Neal's Ashes" and "Please Master" from *Fall of America*,
copyright © 1972 by Allen Ginsberg; "Chances R," "Message II," and "City
Midnight Junk Strains" from *Planet News*, copyright © 1968 by Allen Ginsberg;
"Message" from *Kaddish*, copyright © 1961 by Allen Ginsberg. Reprinted by
permission of City Light Books.

"For great pebbles the beach at Middle Cove (Section VI of "June and July")," "A
Plane to Pittsburgh," and "Like an angel: the piano light" (Section VII of "June
and July") from *Collected Poems* by Paul Goodman, edited by Taylor Stoehr.
Copyright © 1972, 1973 by The Estate of Paul Goodman. Reprinted by permission
of Random House, Inc. "A Hustler" copyright © 1967 by Paul Goodman.
Reprinted from *Collected Poems*, by Paul Goodman, edited by Taylor Stoehr, by
permission of Random House, Inc. "For G., Aet. 16" copyright © 1969, 1970 by
Paul Goodman, reprinted from *Collected Poems*, by Paul Goodman, edited by
Taylor Stoehr, by permission of Random House, Inc.

Harold Norse's "To Mohammed at the Cafe Central," "To Mohammed on Our
Journeys," "To Mohammed at the Hotel of the Palms," "We Bumped Off Your
Friend the Poet," "Island of Giglio," and "You Must Have Been a Sensational
Baby" from *Hotel Nirvana*, copyright © 1974 by Harold Norse. Reprinted by per-
mission of City Lights Books.

Frank O'Hara's "To You" and "Hotel Transylvanie" copyright © 1960; "At the
Old Place" copyright © 1969; "Homosexuality" copyright © 1970—all by
Maureen Granville-Smith, Administratrix of the Estate of Frank O'Hara. Reprinted from *The Collected Poems of Frank O'Hara*, edited by Donald Allen, by
permission of Alfred A. Knopf, Inc.

Czanara's drawing "The Hermaphrodite-Angel of Peladan" reprinted from *The
Other Face of Love* by Raymond de Becker, by permission of Grove Press, Inc.
Copyright © 1969 by Neville Spearman Ltd.

Library of Congress Cataloging in Publication Data
Main entry under title:

Angels of the lyre.

   1. Homosexuality—Poetry. 2. American poetry—20th century. 3. Cana-
dian poetry—20th Century. I. Leyland, Winston. 1940-
PS595.H65A5   811'.5'080353   75-19135
ISBN 0-915572-14-1 lib. bdg.
ISBN 0-915572-13-3 pbk.

Panjandrum Press, Inc.   Gay Sunshine Press
99 Sanchez Street   P.O. Box 40397
San Francisco, Calif. 94114   San Francisco, Calif. 94140

This book was made possible in part by a grant to Panjandrum
Press, Inc., from the National Endowment for the Arts.

Contents

POETRY

7   *Introduction*
13   Hector Tito Alvarez
15   William Barber
19   Bruce Boone
20   Victor Borsa
25   Joe Brainard
30   Perry Brass
32   Adrian Brooks
35   Ira Cohen
38   Kirby Congdon
42   Ed Cox
47   Emilio Cubeiro
49   Tim Dlugos
51   Robert Duncan
54   David Eberly
57   Jim Eggeling
63   Kenward Elmslie
69   Daniel Evans
71   Gerald Fabian
73   Salvatore Farinella
78   Edward Field
81   Charles Henri Ford
85   James Giancarlo
86   Allen Ginsberg
95   John Giorno
101   Robert Gluck
105   Paul Goodman
110   Steve Jonas
115   E. A. Lacey
123   Michael Lally
125   Gerrit Lansing
129   Winston Leyland

132   Gerard Malanga
134   Paul Mariah
142   Wayne McNeill
143   Taylor Mead
148   Thomas Meyer
150   James Mitchell
153   James Nolan
154   Harold Norse
164   Frank O'Hara
169   Chuck Ortleb
171   Stan Persky
174   Robert Peters
180   Vincent Sacardi
182   Ron Schreiber
187   Perry Scott
188   Charley Shively
193   Aaron Shurin
195   David Emerson Smith
197   Jack Spicer
204   George Stanley
205   Richard Tagett
211   Hunce Voelcker
212   John Wieners
224   Jonathan Williams
231   Terence Winch
232   Ian Young
237   *Biographical Notes*
246   *Acknowledgments*

GRAPHICS

2   *Frontispiece:* Aubrey Beardsley: "Androgynous Angel"
62   Wilton David (gleep)
100   Joe Brainard
131   Czanara: "Hermaphrodite-Angel of Peladan"
136   Samuel Reese: prison graphic (lino cut)
179   Edward Aulerich
194   Bruce Reifel: "Gay Brothers & Sisters Unite!"

Cover design by Roger Stearns

Introduction

Gay poetry has a long and rich history and has flourished through the centuries, despite the censorship and bowdlerizing of many scholars and translators. It begins in recorded history three thousand years ago with the *Epic of Gilgamesh* celebrating the love affair between Enkidu and Gilgamesh, and continues with the ancient Greek *Mousa Paidike,* the Roman Catullus, and medieval Arab and Persian poets, through the nineteenth and early twentieth century writers (Whitman, Cavafy, Stefan George, Jean Cocteau, etc.) to the contemporary poets, many of whom have been catalyzed profoundly by the recent Gay Liberation movement.

The fathers of contemporary male Gay poetry are Walt Whitman in the United States and John Addington Symonds in England. Of Whitman much has been written to obfuscate his real consciousness. His homophobic biographers and anthologizers have blatantly ignored or played down his Gayness. Yet homoerotic "adhesive love" was a prominent feature in Whitman's poetry.

Homosexual poets of the 1880's-1890's in England—often called Uranians or Calamites—include Andre Raffalovich, Count Eric Stenbock, Edward Cracroft Lefroy, John Gambril Nicholson, and J. A. Symonds. Most of these poets published in small, limited editions, were read only by a few cognoscenti, and were quickly forgotten. For instance, during his lifetime (1840-1893) Symonds published privately at least sixteen pamphlets of his own poetry, much of it homoerotic in content. Only now are these poets of the Uranian Renaissance being rediscovered and placed in historical perspective.

The trial of Oscar Wilde in 1895 put a brake on the Uranian movement. During the next few decades only a few courageous spirits such as John Moray Stuart-Young and Edmund John published volumes of homoerotic poems. Beginning in the 1920's, the Englishman Ralph Chubb, a recluse who aspired to be a Gay twentieth century William Blake, began to publish through his own press handsomely illustrated volumes in small editions. And a few other poets such as Edwin Emmanuel Bradford and Charles Philip Castle Kains published limited editions of their work.

Generally speaking, however, from the 1930's through the early 1950's it was novelists rather than poets who pioneered in treating homosexual themes. Beginning in the 1950's a few poets began to publish homosexual poetry, and this publishing grew to a small flood by the early 1970's.

In Canada the pioneer was Frank Oliver Call, a university professor of modern languages in Quebec who published, in 1944, a chapbook titled *Sonnets for Youth*. Beginning in the midsixties several Canadian poets began to publish books containing explicitly homoerotic poetry. E. A. Lacey's *The Forms of Loss* (1965) was the first of these. The best known of these Canadian poets is Ian Young, publisher of Catalyst Press, editor of *The Male Muse,* and author of several books of poetry.

In the United States several writers of the late 1950's published poems that were openly Gay in content. For Gay literature the seminal poets of this period are Allen Ginsberg, Frank O'Hara, Jack Spicer, and John Wieners. To the general public, the best known of these poets is Allen Ginsberg, whose long poem "Howl," published in the book of the same name (City Lights, San Francisco, 1956), contains such lines as: "who let themselves be fucked in the ass by saintly motorcyclists, and screamed with joy/ who blew and were blown by those human seraphim, the sailors, caresses of Atlantic and Caribbean love. . . ." But the pioneering book was John Wieners' *Hotel Wentley Poems* (San Francisco, 1958), which includes such titles as "A Poem for Cocksuckers" and "A Poem for the Old Man." The printer of the book was so uptight that he deliberately left out the word "cock" in "Cocksuckers," and a second printing with the unexpurgated title had to be done almost immediately.

The sexual revolution of the 1960's broke down many of the barriers to open expression, and Gay poems appeared in small press books and magazines as well as in such literary journals as *Evergreen Review* and *Avant-Garde* (the latter magazine first published W. H. Auden's pornographic poem "A Day for a Lay").

But for Gay literature the most catalytic event of the 1960's was the New York Stonewall riots of 1969, which sparked off the current Gay Liberation movement. Out of this movement sprang, in 1969–70, several Gay publications (*Gay Sunshine* in Berkeley-San Francisco, *Gay Liberator* in Detroit, *Come Out* in New York City, and, in 1971, Boston's *Fag Rag*). These publications were connected with Gay Liberation Fronts in their respective cities, but from their earliest issues they included some poetry and literary essays by Gay writers.

After the collapse of the GLFs in early 1971 each of these papers underwent a crisis of identity. *Come Out* ceased publication. *Gay Liberator* remained oriented toward political news stories and articles. *Gay Sunshine,* however, evolved into a publication that welcomed and encouraged poetry, literary articles, and graphics (while retaining in-depth political articles). It became, in the words of contemporary composer Lou Harrison, "our major cultural journal." Boston's *Fag Rag* eventually evolved in a similar direction, as did Philadelphia's *Gay Alternative*. Later, in 1974, *Mouth of the Dragon,* a Gay male poetry magazine, commenced publication in New York City; also *Gay Literature* in Fresno, Calif.

For the past four years I have been editor of *Gay Sunshine*. During this time my own interest in poetry and literature impelled me to open up our pages to innovative cultural material by Gay artists and writers and to actively seek such material. I especially encouraged poets to submit their work. Since 1970 we have printed several hundred poems in *Gay Sunshine*—work by well-known poets as well as much work by younger, less-published poets from all over the United States and Canada; and overseas poetry (translations) from Chile, Peru, Japan, and Italy. We have also printed literary/historical essays on such writers as Walter Pater, Steven Jonas, and Constantine Cavafy.

But most significant of all have been the *Gay Sunshine* interviews—a series of in-depth personal conversations (thirteen to date) with such writers and artists as Allen Ginsberg, Christopher Isherwood, Harold Norse, William Burroughs, John Wieners, John Rechy, Ned Rorem, Charles Henri Ford, John Giorno, and Lou Harrison. Most of these interviews have included previously unpublished work by the interviewees.

In early 1972 I began to prepare an anthology of poetry culled from the pages of *Gay Sunshine*. As my work progressed I decided to expand the book to make it a comprehensive anthology of contemporary North American (U.S. and Canada) Gay male poetry. Panjandrum Press, a San Francisco alternative small press, agreed to publish the anthology jointly with *Gay Sunshine*. As a male I did not feel competent to anthologize women's poetry. This is being done by women themselves in such books as *This Is Women's Work* and *We Are All Lesbians*.

Forty-five of the fifty-seven poets in this anthology have had work published in *Gay Sunshine,* and many of the poems in the present book originally appeared in our journal. Others appeared in publications such as *Fag Rag, Manroot, Sebastian Quill,* and *Mouth of the Dragon.* All of the poems printed here were written within the last twenty-five years—most of them within the last decade—a fertile period for the new wave of American and Canadian poetry. Only five of the poets included are deceased (Spicer, O'Hara, Goodman, Jonas, Sacardi). Almost all have been published extensively in small press magazines and have had one or more books or chapbooks of poems printed. The age range of contributors is quite wide, from 22 to 62.

The title of the anthology, *Angels of the Lyre,* reflects in part that fact that I have been, like Jean Cocteau, a life-long angelophile. Interestingly, there are a disproportionate number of contemporary Gay poems with angel themes or motifs. The lyre, of course, is the harp-like stringed instrument that was used by the ancient Greeks for accompanying song and recitative. The word is also used in a figurative sense as the symbol of lyric poetry. And in Greek mythology the sun-god Apollo, patron of music and poetry, was adept on the lyre, no doubt using it to charm his lover, Hypnos. The musician Orpheus, son of Apollo, was said to be able to move rocks and trees by the power of his lyre. According to one of the Orphic myths, Orpheus went to Thrace and started a cult of boy-love there.

The present volume with its fifty-seven poets and 248 pages is the most comprehensive collection of contemporary Gay poetry to date, and I hope it will be considered a pioneering work. But due credit must also be given to five precursor anthologies.

The first of these, Edward Carpenter's *Iolaus: An Anthology of Friendship,* was published in England as long ago as 1902 and contained work by Roman and Greek poets in addition to nineteenth century poets such as Tennyson, Swinburne, William Johnson Cory, and Walt Whitman.

In 1924 there was published in New York a slim (84 pages)

privately printed volume titled *Men and Boys: An Anthology.* This now very rare volume of Uranian poetry (only 150 copies were printed) included work by forty-nine American and British poets, many of them obscure even to this day. The editor is given as "Edmund Edwinson," but this is almost certainly a pseudonym. The real editor may have been Reginald Bancroft Cooke, the American translator of Platen.

The third work, *Eros: An Anthology of Friendship* (1961), edited by Patrick Anderson and Alistair Sutherland, expands Carpenter's anthology and brings it up to date. Included are writings (prose and poetry) from ancient Israel through the Greek, Roman, and medieval periods to the present day. Very little contemporary (post-World War II) poetry is given, however. The editorial introduction is rather coy: its seven pages of discussion about male-to-male love/friendship are devoid of the words homosexual or homosexuality.

In 1970 Brian Reade edited a volume *Sexual Heretics: Male Homosexuality in English Literature from 1850 to 1900.* Fifty-six pages of scholarly introduction is followed by almost four hundred pages of prose and poetry—all on homosexual themes—from major and minor British Victorian writers.

The fifth precursor volume is Ian Young's 129-page collection *The Male Muse,* published by Crossing Press (Trumansburg, N.Y., 1973). This is the first contemporary Gay poetry anthology. Included are forty poets, British, American, and Canadian. With the exceptions of Jay Socin and Paul Goodman, no deceased poets are included; such seminal poets as Spicer, Jonas, and O'Hara were passed over.

The two pioneering books on the lives and work of Gay poets are Rupert Croft-Cooke's *Feasting with Panthers* (New York, 1967), a witty, gossipy account of several late Victorian writers such as Symonds, Wilde, Swinburne, and Whitman; and Timothy d'Arch Smith's erudite *Love in Earnest,* subtitled "Some Notes on the Lives and Writings of English Uranian Poets from 1889 to 1930" (London, 1970). Valuable information on Gay literature from 1930 to the present is included in the interviews with literary figures (mentioned above) which have appeared in each issue of *Gay Sunshine* since Number 16 (January 1973). An anthology of these interviews, edited by myself, will appear in 1976.

Most of the poets I approached for contributions to the present anthology were extremely cooperative, and I thank them for their kindness and generosity. Two or three poets declined to be included because they claimed there was no such thing as Gay Poetry and they didn't want to be categorized. My intention in compiling this collection, however, was not to divide poets into Gay and straight. Several of the writers included here are in fact bisexual, and almost none write poems that are exclusively Gay in content. Yet, there is such a thing as Gay Sensibility, just as there are Black, Chicano, and Indian sensibilities. This Gay Sensibility is more refined in certain poets than in others. For instance, all of John Wieners' and Frank O'Hara's work is imbued with a gay *élan vital,* even though only a handful of the latter's poems are on explicitly Gay themes. My own criteria in choosing poems for this anthology were (1) poetical skill/high quality of writing; (2) whether or not each poem chosen is imbued, directly or indirectly, with a Gay sensibility.

I think one important truth illustrated by the poems printed here is that Gayness extends far beyond physical sexuality. There are many dimensions to Gayness, and especially since Stonewall, poets have been exploring the subtleties of these dimensions. I believe the present anthology contains many examples of this exploration: see, for instance, the poems by Shurin, Persky, and Mariah. And for more than one poet Stonewall was a catalyst for a creative Gay "coming out." For example, in 1972 Harold Norse submitted several poems on Gay themes to *Gay Sunshine* (which were printed in the journal); some of these had been written a decade or more earlier, and the poet felt that the time and place had finally come for their publication.

I hope that the next decade will see even deeper poetic explorations springing from heightened Gay consciousness and awareness.

My thanks to all who helped make this anthology possible, especially to Charley Shively, Ian Young, Paul Mariah, and Adrian Brooks, for their kind assistance.

Winston Leyland
San Francisco
Spring 1975

Hector Tito Alvarez

THE BIRTH OF THE POLITICAL ANGEL

oceans, as if space were
apples,
the scent of oranges,
marcos naked
fields and fields of clear grey-blue,
lilac on white.
the chalk
hills and breasts filled with milk
images, blue crystal in the snow,
Indians in the snow
Indians in the snow
bleached, clean flakes on the white linen
                              (original Mind)

or paint/blood
applied with the grace of the greeks;
graceful lines in the snow
gay patterns in the sun's labyrinth
upright, green stems bleeding,
his firm thigh
in the sun
how men with men are one
my loving when
well, men are as flowers,
pebbles in the stream, not boulders

when pablo as
surrendering in the snow
flowing off the white pages
coming, buttermilk dripping on tissue paper
forfeiting muscles and metal teeth
balls and power, metallic balls
shining chrome in the snow

in the powdered universe of northern lights
                                                    Mts.
and opening his warmth as if space were,
                              every pine were his.
latino, blond, and grey eyes tender
colored shells on the cuban sand, moist.
Breath,
as with marcos breathing gently;
planes and plains filled with Indians
Indians in the Alps of the north country.
blue
coming, clear brooks

blocks of sparkling ice
Lorca, crying in the snow
(como un gallo)
stalactites and stalagmites
and phalloi carved out of cave walls
ancient space for living: sculpting
                              painting
                              fucking
                              thinking
ancient grace of brotherly embrace
in the blanched snow
in the snow
men loving men
as if our own bodies were space enough

"Oh, words and spices are for the dead, anyway!"

1974 nyc

William Barber

THE GAY POET

I have broken the sound barrier of morality
with one crunchy bite on the phallic biscuit.
In my boyish womanhood, with my soul in drag,
I have been personal concubine to hundreds
of queens and princes, mistress of many
hedonists, lover of all.

I have pricked, prodded, pampered and pumped,
held my knees to my ears in the amyl twilight
and gone totally and obtusely mad, because
one halfway beautiful man weighed
a thousand tons on my fragile psyche.
My anima is stripped by the sight of my
wrinkled ego hanging out his back pocket
always two steps ahead of me.

I will go on, unknown lovers in my future,
I will be there. waiting with my mouth in my hand
to show you the ways into my body/being.
curling my wits to help you laugh out your orgasms,
but I am totally insane
because one of you, one too many of you
walked out that morning with all my reason
crumpled inside your tawny levis.

A FUCK POEM IN THE TRADITION OF REALITY

for Gerry Fabian

"A man who will wear white mukluks will do anything!"
                                                —*Bradley*

Yes he was gorgeous and danced like a hot bull
hauling through town. In the black-walled bar
that swings like Rio, yes the dancehall,
the baboon's favorite tree, Fabian,
(because you wanted to know what happened)
I was out of cigarettes and in love.

Yes he took me to his house that was a tent
with a painted parachute ceiling
and muslin circular walls, saying:
"I have a carton of Camels. I'll give you a pack
to smoke before and after on the mattresses."
A sheik, or chic, or cheeks, a moving statue's body.
I gave him my legs and arms like clay mallets
and our backs and asses twisted all night
long.

So when I woke in the morning and lay still an hour
watching his sleeping, I gradually talked myself
out of that wish to stay there, repeating it.
I've learned the grapes, how each morning
is a new morning, how surfaces heal. The only thing
he saw me take with me was the Camels.
I smoked them for a day, to cover the empty spaces.

Yet this week when I saw him again, outside the bar
someone else was admiring his mukluks.
I was in a doorway dodging the rain, they didn't see me
as they crossed in front of me. But I heard
a slice of dialogue that was the real fucking.
I heard the bull boy say to the new face:
"I have a carton of Camels. I'll give you a pack."

HUSTLER JOE

Joe is going back to Arkansas, says its "on account" his
Dad's sick and his brother has a job building boats and
drives a Cougar. At the hotel, Joe paid his bill by selling sections of his pink flesh to San Francisco on the wide
meat highway. Said it was a pain in the ass. "Course,
so's the war" he said, preferring women. Yet old Joe really
gave a man his money's worth; he'd roll either way, fag
fucking, nothing to it but a little hurting, nothing to a
mouthful of hot jizz, even an old man's jizz, so long's he's
    paying.

We was buddies, me and Joe. I'd screw him before he'd go
out, just to get him loose, for his consumers. At night,
sometimes, he'd blow me if the lights were out. Such a
pretty face, real blond hair, marine cut, the "shits" and
"jesuses" completely natural. Ten dollars hid in the bible,
six in his pocket, on the prowl. Joe walked through rain
like it wasn't raining, looked at a green wall and a torn shade
and saw only his thoughts, beer, broads, the open road.

Tomorrow morning he'll take the greyhound to Fayetteville,
the Ozark mountains. They said $44.25 for a one way ticket.
I gave him ten dollars for a ride on his back, dreaming of
horses on the green slopes of Appalachia, but he was still
$25.00 short. He pulled up his pants and we said goodbye
forever I guess, and he was back on the street in his blue
snugs with his big smile, so available. If interested,
please write to this poem, care of the wind, because by now
Joe's been gone so long he's fathered his own kids in Arkansas.

SERIAL POEM

Last night I dreamed
                    I jumped
from the brown cliff
into a circle of blue water,

and it was good and cool
and I had broken from you
at last.

I supposed I dreamed of tricks
churning my vision
like minnows,

And I went swimming toward them
beneath the surface.

When I woke you were gone.

Tonight your arms
                    are holding down
a younger boy,
and your mouth is a river
flowing into his skin
with the passion
of our first night.

Bruce Boone

HE'S THE *LOVER* / OF MY *SOUL*

Suddenly I am thinking of Francis,
which is a sissy name and the name
                              of the one
I remember (why?) in the sixth grade
he wet his pants
                    we were in love and catholics
we were always looking back fondly and sadly
because catholics always do
                          we were looking back
as sissies do

              yet we were in love

all the world loves a lover
                          but does it
when their names are Bruce and Francis?
we showed it by chasing girls
                          and tearing their clothes
but we carved our names on the sacred heart
we knew the language of flowers
                              and aside from us
they only talked to girls
                          filling the glorious
churches of our hearts
                    making us gasp for breath
for the blueness of the sky
                        where love shot out
the flame, the choir, and all that heaven ever gave
it gave us to think
                    we were in the second grade again
as proud as kings
                    and I remember running down the hall
                    and all the girls would run
for the grief and joy

Victor Borsa

THE FEEL OF TEETH

not like snapping mongrel
nor north wind cruel
upon your face
is the feel of teeth
of your lover

there's something of flowers
when frost scars their bleeding
skins—predawn of October,
a gathering of roots

I call it hawk wing
in midnight winter   beak
upon my flesh in pause
of flight

music to break stillness
of a Sunday morning
(Russian as in
balalaika
wild
as in honey)

first then the lips and preliminary
drowning in arms
the drifting grass   burning
of hunger

yes and finally the pain
of teeth of your fine
barbarian love.

(Taste me gentle and be wild
and let me feel the color
of our flight)

I SPEAK WITH MY ANGEL

I speak with you tonight because
midnight is a guillotine of dreams
I must avoid   you lead
when stars are dark
to brighter moons

you are beautiful, angel, omnipresent
in this gasp of time—
you see what I cannot,
know what I do not
understand

guardian angel I speak with eyes
that are rivers of words only you
can hear   look at my eyes
tonight and answer me
to ecstasy of peace

there are such terrors just steps
outside my door   tigers
yellowing the night like marigolds:
mock gardens that I dare
not stroll

see the serpents there, floating
in the tropics of my heart
see the awful murder of love
by solitude, the fury
of fallen eyes

see the city burning, angel,
the suicide of yearning flesh—
guard me angel, with your voice
and with your body;
I speak
          to you tonight

YOUNG MAN DANCING

The sign reads
'groove but do not
dance'

nonetheless the emphatic
angel within you bends
to rhythmic runaway

and fresh you birth
absolute with motion
in rising allegro

(a game of lyric baseball
with tempos aiming
at your blood)

'do not dance' the sign
reads and disparate men groove
obedient in static furniture

of their bones,
close around, and mutter darkly:
'do not dance'

    (will the city crumble?
     will the universe fall?)

You smile, your energy vector
beams outward, spreads
your singular choreography past walls

like strongest sun. Men grown fear-
ful will not float
on luminous waves, angel—

    Still your torso,
       your arms and legs.
    We have too much
    of madness here
    we will have more
    of death.

Young man dancing, it is enough.
Your jubilant language
will jeopardize our quilted stance.

Groove inward, angel—
do not dance.

THE SOUND

listen to the sound of growing
old   the clock's ticking play
ground is your skin your hair
your hands your eyes

look into the mirror as day
wears on. See the growing
shadows of your mind reflected
on your face. See the almost
invisible scars.

the earth now has a discern-
ible sphere, thunder is no longer drama
but science   red is only color; there
is no urgency to fire engines

there is something dancing in your dreams
that remembers you are still
alive   you explore
the memory of a love. It becomes
more real than your waking
or your death

                you remember
the sound of love, the moon
is in your blood. Your body stirs,
you can only hear
                the wind

pseudo woman in your dark joy
at Gene Comptons, miniskirted and pink
inverting sexes with urgency
in frills and bracelets and finger—

nail polish; Nefertiti now blond profiled
of flowing brow and sloe-eyed stare
in desperate argument against masc-
ulinity, you play with coke and destiny

alike, measuring your words
and lines with studied softness, aware
of men pondering your feminacy.
Being a woman is more important now

than Life itself; recalcitrant you sit
in radiance calculated of desire, fighting
your violated self with love. To whore
is suddenly ultimate and beautiful:
you kiss

a passing leatherboy with your eyes

Joe Brainard

I REMEMBER [*selections*]

I remember when, in high school if you wore green and yellow on Thursday it meant that you were queer.

I remember when, in high school I used to stuff a sock in my underwear.

I remember "queers can't whistle."

I remember the skinny guy who gets sand kicked in his face in body-building ads.

I remember how much I used to stutter.

I remember how little your dick is getting out of a wet bathing suit.

I remember daydreams of a doctor who (on the sly) was experimenting with a drug that would turn you into a real stud. All very "hush-hush." (As it was illegal.) There was a slight chance that something might go wrong and that I'd end up with a really *giant* cock, but I was willing to take that chance.

I remember my first sexual experience in a subway. Some guy (I was afraid to look at him) got a hardon and was rubbing it back and forth against my arm. I got very excited and when my stop came I hurried out and home where I tried to do an oil painting using my dick as a brush.

I remember when I had a job cleaning out an old man's apartment who had died. Among his belongings was a very old photograph of a naked young boy pinned to an old pair of young boy's underwear. For many years he was the choir director at church. He had no family or relatives.

I remember how many other magazines I had to buy in order to buy one physique magazine.

I remember jerking off to sexual fantasies of Troy Donahue with a dark tan in a white bathing suit down by the ocean. (From a movie with Sandra Dee)

I remember sexual fantasies of seducing young country boys. (But old enough) Pale and blond and eager.

I remember the way John Kerr was always flexing his jaw muscles in "South Pacific."

I remember that Rock Hudson and Charlie Chaplin and Lyndon Johnson have "giant cocks."

I remember magazine pictures of very handsome male models with perfect faces and, with an almost physical pang, wondering what it would be to look like that. (Heaven)

I remember those sexy little ads in the back of *Esquire* magazine of skimpy bathing suits and underwear with enormous baskets.

I remember the first time I met Frank O'Hara. He was walking down Second Avenue. It was a cool early Spring evening but he was wearing only a white shirt with the sleeves rolled up to his elbows. And blue jeans. And moccasins. I remember that he seemed very sissy to me. Very theatrical. Decadent. I remember that I liked him instantly.

I remember Frank O'Hara's walk. Light and sassy. With a slight bounce and a slight twist. It was a beautiful walk. Confident. "I don't care." And sometimes "I know you are looking."

I remember seeing Frank O'Hara write a poem once. We were watching a western on TV and he got up as tho to fix a drink or answer the telephone but instead he went over to the typewriter, leaned over it a bit, and typed for 4 or 5 minutes standing up. Then he pulled the piece of paper out of the typewriter and handed it to me and then lay back down to watch more TV. (The TV was in the bedroom) I don't remember the poem except that it had some cowboy dialect in it.

I remember not liking myself for not picking up boys I probably could pick up because of the possibility of being rejected.

I remember deciding at a certain point that I would cut

through all the bull shit and just go up to boys I liked and say "Do you want to go home with me?" and so I tried it. But it didn't work. Except once, and he was drunk. The next morning he left a card behind with a picture of Jesus on it signed "with love, Jesus" on the back. He said he was a friend of Allen Ginsberg.

I remember tight white pants. Certain ways of standing. Blond heads of hair. And spotted bleached blue jeans.

I remember pretty faces that don't move.

I remember (recently) getting blown while trying to carry on a normal conversation on the telephone, which, I must admit, was a big turn-on somehow.

I remember fantasizing about being a super-stud and being able to shoot *enormous* loads. And (would you believe it?) ((yes, you'll believe it)) I still do.

PORNOGRAPHIC MOVIE PLOT CAPSULE NO. 7
(A FEATURE)

Midnight finds us under the stars under an army blanket under another army blanket (it's cold outside) in Vietnam. Two young blond soldiers, each from a different middle state, are going at each other full steam ahead when, in a nearby tent, the "Sarge" gets up to take a leak. Two possibilities present themselves here: a threesome featuring a piss sequence, or a "court martial--S & M--prison" montage.

PORNOGRAPHIC MOVIE PLOT CAPSULE NO. 11
(A DOUBLE-FEATURE)

FEATURE NO. 1

An expensive private school just a few hours outside London finds two little boys exposing themselves to each other behind a bush, as two head-masters are looking on from a third story window, jerking each other off into baggies so the maids, busy creaming each other simultaneously with brooms in the broom closet (it's a big broom closet) won't find any tell-tale clues. While unbeknownst to all, the mysterious dean (an inventor at heart) is watching all these various activities (including the gardener and his cute ex-son-in-law assistant, which is a whole other story I assure you) ((The second feature of this double-feature)) on his newest invention: a viewing screen that picks up everything that goes on within a one mile radius. The dean, as understanding as he is mysterious, calls everybody in for "reprimands" (a dungeon fantasy scene here, with whips and chains, etc.) fully enjoyed by one and all.

FEATURE NO. 2

Potting up some petunias in the greenhouse the gardener runs across a fingernail with a bit of flesh dangling from it amid his potting soil. The gardener, a suspicious man by nature, suspecting that it may be the lead he's been waiting for in the mysterious disappearance of his daughter three months ago, approaches his cute ex-son-in-law assistant, Stud, with the smelly piece of evidence. Stud, hung like a horse, staggers. Somewhat shaken, but hung like a horse, Stud quickly regains his composure, unzips his pants, and out plops the biggest dong this side, or any side, of Texas. They live happily (use your imagination here) ever after.

PORNOGRAPHIC MOVIE PLOT CAPSULE NO. 12
(A SHORT)

A thirteen year old Puerto Rican drag queen is not putting up *too* much resistance being raped by a big burly hairy rapist among the autumn leaves (crunch-crackle-crunch-crunch-crackle) in Fun City's Central Park U.S.A.

PORNOGRAPHIC MOVIE PLOT CAPSULE NO. 14
(A SHORT)

As Mrs. Jones is pondering the habitual disappearance of her little Johnny's underwear, the not yet married choir director next door is slipping yet another pair of little Johnny's underwear into his smelly bottom dresser drawer, as little Johnny zips up his pants with a crisp new one dollar bill clutched in his left paw, and walks out the back door preparing a big question mark on his face to confront his poor dear dumb perplexed mother with.

PORNOGRAPHIC MOVIE PLOT CAPSULE NO. 15
(A SHORT)

A cute French sailor, in port for only a few hours, is pulling his tight white trousers down over his chunky ass as a fart escapes from inbetween his two white buns right into the face of another cute French sailor, also in port for only a few hours, who, as luck would have it, really gets off on farts in the face.

PORNOGRAPHIC MOVIE PLOT CAPSULE NO. 18
(AN "ART" SHORT)

A Negro young man and an Albino young man (take advantage here of "contrast") are making love out on a raft in the middle of the ocean under a big blue sky which turns into a fantastic orange sunset simultaneously with "climax."

Perry Brass

IN LOVING YOU

In loving you,
I have loved all men.
I see them walking down the street
rainbow-eyed,   flower heads
stalk-necked   flowers of energy
and I have loved all men loving you
holding your face in my hands
I see all men

but in your face I see
only your eyes

I wanted you to be
what I was not
I wanted you to be friend
and father and lover and adventureful pal
companion to my sleepless nights, evening
fairy who sneaks up the bedroom stairs
into my waiting nakedness, when I am tired
of the games and doubts of men.

FAIRY

the word fairy has been much abused
it is a word
of soft flight and breath
of Ariel's tenderness
Pan fantasy   unexpected kindness

when I was a freshman going to school in Georgia
a long time ago, my friend
Franklin and I trudged
up the hill to McDonald's
to eat hamburgers late at night when a lot
of frat boys were there. One was talking
to his friends, "I took her out
all night and still did not get to fuck her,"
then he saw me and Franklin and
looked at me and I just smiled
and he said, "now y'all have a good time
flying home, ya see."

I THINK THE NEW TEACHER'S
A QUEER

"I think the new teacher's a queer,"

I turned around
and saw that
they were talking about me,

one false move
and it would be over,
I could not drop my wrists
or raise my voice

so I stood there up against the board
arms folded
pressed against my chest
and looked out without seeing
or hearing until
the children became a noiseless pattern

and all those years
from when I sat among them
stopped dead and I feared
that they'd beat me up

in the boy's room.

Adrian Brooks

"YES"

when you touched my hair and I said yes   go on
you touched my cheek and I thought
how glad I am it's smooth   go on
you put your hand behind my neck
fell back against your palm—
one fiftieth of a boa constrictor
lying in your hand as you move and
touch my breast which calls
invisible birds to rise and
nipples stand to attention
when you go down
brush my stomach   go on
to undo buttons with one hand
could turn it side to side
and faster moves in
to meet my arms
like very wise snakes
coiled around the river valley
running up your back to your head
lying on the flat country
mouth open and ready to   go on
take me into wet
curtains close over
and push up from below
and I am a snake in the river   go on
you are the current and yes
I was, I am   go on
I will.

August 21, 1974
San Francisco

[Untitled]

Here is the queen
getting ready for a party.
He stands in the bathroom
pinning a flower in his hair.
It is a silk rose.
He touches his collarbone—
ascertains its definition:
He will wear something
with a low front.
At the mirror
he powders his face.
He surveys it like virgin land
ready for development.
He pencils thin brows
and views his progress.
There's a lot to do.
Our queen must leave in five minutes.
He adds green to the eyelids,
finds the rouge and colors
the white base.
The queen stands back:
He darkens the lips.
He decides the rose is too much
and adds rhinestone clips.
It's starting to work.
The eyes darken—
lines are extended.
Quick dabs of sandalwood
at the wrist, elbow and neck—
It's getting *hot*.
A vamp replaces the country lass
(not for the first or last time).
One minute to touch down
the queen slips into a white satin dress
and brushes his hair
away from his face.
Transformation is complete.

A creature of the night
ready to enter the neon arena
picks up the raincoat
throws it over the satin dress
and trips out the door
on his way toward the glory of sidewalks
and the light of passing cars.

Out on the street
the queen moves between lamplight
and shadows
as if drawn to a magnet
invisible to the naked eye.
If you listen carefully
you can hear the rustle of a gown
on castle stairs—
the wheels of imaginary carriages
rattling along cobblestone streets
toward a fatal rendez-vous.
The queen cruises past the donut shop.
His legs—inside the satin gown—
are coming alive.
His body is electric again
he is living cinema—
only distantly related
to this century.

CIRCUS
───────────

Middle aged queers and I
share a silent joke;
the lines on their faces
look like the nets
into which I shall fall
when my trapeze artist face
loses star billing
and moves from the center ring.

Ira Cohen

[*Untitled*]

for P.V.

But what in your other hand lies concealed?
    this gift that I give you
    this laughter
    this exquisite geometry
    these dangling lines
      the skulls & wires
      seen thru a glass
      the light as it turns
      out of itself
this scene that will pass
this hand which encircles
        this flame
        this silver dust
     this song which will last
       this scorpion whip
       this silver tip
     this play we play
      this instant
       in our hand
     this pain in your heart
     these lips I understand
     this precious beast
      made of teeth & roses
& you are this play
& this play never ends
& you are this play
& this play never ends
  this shadow which
  neither of us understands
    between the days
     of ecstasy & betrayal

The female impersonator
sits for a portrait before
the wig is carried in
by three assistants
In the mouth
a subtle twist of
expression
betrays a gulf of separation
(Heads cut from bodies of bandits
falling on terraces of SNOW)
A flower is dropped and
the courtesan hidden
behind a wall of fans
knows what is expected
of her
knows what it is
to be a thing
moving in rooms
a beaten heart beating/
Utaemon sits in the wings
Oblivious
while an ancient spirit
pale & forever unfulfilled
walks across the RAMP
in wooden clogs
carrying a parasol . . .
Will you change into a butterfly
again?
& this subtle knot—
does it untie itself
in a heap of falling silk
as you stand w/yr back
to the audience?
I see you under a dry leaf
immaculate as a caterpillar
cleaning its feet—there
on the other side of the mirror

where you eat your rice
    w/out EYEBROWS!

[*Untitled*]
_____

for Dana

              Hidden treasure
Lying down w/the orchid
faced dancer in a explosion
                of fur
You fall thru the trapdoor
   of opium followed by
   the enigmatic bundle
      flying without hands or feet
         so close behind you
If the candle is your wand
If you wear the face of OBSESSION
If the slumbering image has
      been cut by scissors
you will know that while
   you are sleeping
   the sun is spinning gold
   into the earth &
   that you are climbing
   without steps
I pull apart my pillow
in search of feathers &
discover that the photograph
   of the Alchemist
   has fallen unnoticed
      from the violin case
scarcely a thousand paces
   eastward of the temple gate
You remain frozen
   in the attitude of
   a fountain
about to awaken
            dormant
               stones
greedy of windows

Kirby Congdon

JAGANNATH

. . . and when, after years of developing it, he had molded every contour of his body to perfection, marveling in the cold mirror the taut curves of the pectorals, the lean, hard undulations of his abdomen, and the restrained power of his swollen thighs, with hypnotic fascination—almost greed—in his eyes, he pushed his middle finger under his testicles, into his rectum and pressed forward. So, he ejaculated before the mirror, and as often as possible. His eyes gobbled up all the different and perfected sections of his straining body until, throwing his head back, and rising on his toes, his pelvis shoved forward, the semen jerked out like his very soul, arching in space, thick in its glorious waste, uniting itself with the empty air like far-flung and briefly luminous constellations which fell in their destruction with soft splats against the mirror and onto the floor until he doubled over in exhaustion and then leaned, breathing heavily, against the wall and watched his body slowly relax its magnificent tensions.

He exercised and manipulated his beauty every day, sharing it only in the sidelong glance of strangers who watched his athletic movements or caught a glimpse of his body which revealed itself as a living explication of the human form—to be handled and coddled and toyed with, roughed about and teased and mistreated until that body broke in its purest function and lay, still beautiful, like a great imaginary landscape, with a thigh or a breastplate glistening with his own body's juice where, far-flung, it had landed and was just beginning to leak out from its own heavy substance, to define a muscle's shape like a painful tear. Obsessed with himself, he was happy to enjoy the workings of his interior body, to have those strange unknown motors move, run, churn and race, pumping up a wellful of compressed sludge until this volcano of lava vomited up his very loins under the studied, shameless gaze of his one admirer in the mirror.

But now he found a silent place in a desert area, on a hill-top close to heaven which looked down on him with its great indifferent eye, pretending not to care or to watch, as he removed his clothes. Lying down, he inserted the gun barrel into his rectum and aggravated himself in an almost ugly and mean fashion, his fist on his erect cock, stroking and twisting it cruelly over and over again to the breaking point, releasing his hand just quickly enough to forestall an ejaculation, as the head of the penis alternately shone with its anticipatory lubricant.

Finally, as the afternoon wore on, he knew it was time. He rested until all was quiet and relaxed so that he could appreciate the full sweep of his excitement. He began slowly and forced himself not to rush his progress, and then he attacked his cock roughly, occasionally rolling over, the gravel scrubbing his driving-rod knuckles raw and the gun barrel jabbing his rectum compulsively. His throat clutched at the air in gasps as he felt his loins convulse at the center of his being. The throbs sped through his fingers where the semen rushed through his flaming cock in hard pellets. As the first glob seemed to push his thighs apart with its force, his cock broke out of his blinded hand and as the second burst fell on his body like fireworks, he pulled the trigger of the other gun. Its one expensive bullet lunged its way deep into his stomach without time, and blasted a white hole that seemed larger than his own torso for the length of his prostrate body. His penis continued to break forth in ruptured joy until at last it subsided, and he was left for the rest of the afternoon bathed in his own sweat, under his own semen, and on top of his own blood, under the impassive sky which looked down on him as indifferently as before.

His pain lifted him out of himself, his brain a mass of shapeless fire, a molten, boiling stone of hideous sensitivity and feeling that swarmed over him and advanced and retreated like the sun moving in and out of focus, or like galaxies of time itself exploding and shrinking in the slow motions of astronomical speeds. In time, before the sun itself had set, he died.

When his admirer came from out of his mirror and found the corpse, he saw the position of the gun and understood. He looked close and saw where the semen had dried in shallow, almost invisible scabs on his still body. The visitor knelt down on the ground beside the body, withdrew his cock, waited dispassionately for it to grow full and large, and then covered the suicide once more with medallions of come. Then he removed his own clothes and lay down naked with the corpse for a while, chest to chest. Having regained his strength, he put his clothes back on and headed down the hill toward the town and the people.

It was a beautiful day, filled with love. It was holy and the people in it seemed, all of them, to be saints. And the dying and the dead—martyrs whom he alone had blessed and whose transfiguration he alone had witnessed, and whose meaninglessness he alone knew—had more meaning than existence itself—an existence which was the fulfillment of life into the very extremes of its far-flung boundaries, which are those far-off yet so close frontiers of death.

SUNS

In nothingness,
the sun's hot body cannot float;
to nothingness, does not sink,
but suspends itself
in circles of self-sustained balloons.
My body is tied to gravity.
My bones are magnetized
and hard as iron.
Yet this body knows
its high-timed origins,
and, in praise of noon,
leans upward towards the source of heaven
and in that land of plenty
blooms.

HORSE-OPERA

His very victims
also overcome,
drunk with death,
prostrate,
and past ecstasy,
the cowboy-hero, cool,
blows smoke
from his hot gun's barrel
that banged his leather-vested
partner/villain
down to dust,
and tucks the rod away
like a still-stiff cock
that's just shot off
its stinging load
into the second-man's entrails
and marries,
in love's hate,
and war's own peace,
his mirror's mate;
re-enacts a myth,
a play of words,
a game of wish
and all of it
hides love's hard kiss.

MOTORCYCLIST

The intoxicating stench of gas
mixes with the body's sweat
and smell of musk.
Their leather torsos,
riding iron bulls,
intimate and crouched,
intense in the lover's act,
copulate with their hot machines.
Blood and oil are one.
They eat and digest
death.

Ed Cox

WAKING

could feel breath
on neck stiffness
at side   pull you slowly
through sleep to waking
to face   your cock
close to lips   not touching
mouth soft   round onto you
vein of underside
in throat slowly mouth wet
slowly pushing into my mouth
again motion wet
hands hold your ass slowly
tight cock in throat wet
pulling you from me small
opening close to mouth not touching
hard, length motion
of hands to you pulling motion
in hand you bend head back
upright slowly you bend back
in motion to let go so close
to my lips not touching
your breathing becoming other sound
hand, hair, face, sleep comes
from inside comes fast
from inside of you   out onto
face my face is warm I am
gasping for air my mouth wet
taste of sky we were biking
along canal there were clusters
of rock in river of morning, of you
now on my face   clear, wide sky

how we can give to each other

THREE IN THE MORNING

The stillness is thick.
Dark covers door and corner—
the wall a blind gallery:
paintings without frame or face.

You are awake
while others sleep.

This is the time,
moment only you share,
when you unbutton your shirt,
touch your chest—
your hand an earth in itself
moving so sure, so slow.

Light rises between your fingers.

CRUISING

someone will come up
approach you on the street
and say
I haven't been here long
this place,   this way
this wind,   these windows

I.

All night the river draws tight.
The Bridge looms wide,
                          green steel,
Brackish,
          the cords drawn to ice,
Breath inching,
          pushing out at all sides.

II.

This would be a place
Where you would walk,   dark,
No cadence,
No climbing rush to trains,
In a cord of place
That brings towns,   early hours,
Strolls home,
Those quick cruises to the docks.

All here, the green rising,
Stretched out over the Hudson.
Bridge, you.
Light off the Coast of Mexico:
Lost cord, Phrase
And you a poem,   Always.

III.

What is to be learned from you?:
The twenties. Names of presidents
I don't care to remember, recall,
Out of text their prohibitions
Driving you to riskier bars
Where men
                if an eye flash
Stood out   cords on a Bridge   a gap.

That Bridge as wide in your room
As your words trafficking back and forth:
Train, Bridge, your name—
                              the constant
                              traveller—
The lone walk: Bar, Bridge, and Ships:

You: engulfed,
Afraid as all of us.

WINDOWS

rain   wake to
breathing of a friend, Bobbie,
his head   brown hair
and sitting up   to see his neck
wanting him to move,
                              pull back covers
his legs,
          cock I wanted to touch
even while he would sleep
                              & me shaking
erect, moon, leaf, smell of his body
wanting him to stir
                    slow
afraid as me to touch
be together in dark
through walls
door shutting two flights up

WAITING

I've no idea, sense of place,
where you might be when you stare out
across this crowded bar. Your eyes
have found some space I can not see:
rooms you've slept in, long streets,
the face of a man you've met here before.

You keep your head down, look up only
when the sound of the door opens
or closes over the song someone has played
three times. In ten minutes
you've pulled the blue plaid cuff
of your shirt sleeve twice to check the time.
It's late. I could tell you that.

We wait, stall for this person
we believe—tell ourselves,
write in letters to distant friends,—
will walk in, sit down, and turning
hear the words we find in our hands.

ROOM

we go into   after getting out of car
morning walk up stairs
when we sit,   fall

touching, just touching
blood goes to where it will then
stillness between legs, neck relaxes
veins: arms, legs cock
body inside has curves, places wet

Emilio Cubeiro

"YES, I'M LIVING ON" #XXIX

I impress myself I do
I am inspired by me I can do
I am always given inspiration I shall do
as I am told
whatever you my master desire
I am yours
my heart beats for you
my lungs are yours especially since you smoke
    two packs a day that is why I stopped smoking
    so I can give you a lung when you lay dying
    and I say no to the cosmos and give you my lung
    and I am a martyr granted sainthood by all
    true visionaries of the masturbatory arts
my hair so dark and silky is for your fingers
my penis harder in intensity than in looks is for your majesty
my chest is for you to lie on
my nipples belong to you but don't start thinking
    of buying me gold earrings because I don't wear
    any jewels even if I shouldn't be telling you
    what to do but then again the slave is really
    the master here in a conscious sexual fantasy
    but not so in the subterranean realms of those
    in the political slave and master playground
    for here the sandbox contains gold
and my ass, my ass really rarely penetrated
    I give it to you   it is yours
    take me where you will
    it awaits your stab your pierce of
    vengeful oh so beautifully vindictive
    lustful passionate contempt-like
    thrusts containing and element of love

and my hands   they have been consecrated with
    musical ability   let me play on your
    body as one would on a harpsichord
and my eyes that see through you to your core
    boring with drill-like precision to examine the essence
insult me   call me names   use outrageous words
show me you love me or hate me or
you love me and hate me but do something to me
use your imagination go ahead you can   relax
feel free and uninhibited   tell me what your wildest thought
    ever was   I won't tell anybody
    yes   yes and do you think of that a lot
I'm not into physical pain but you can beat me anyway
I'll do anything for you   I told you
if you want to kill me I won't try and stop you
    but may I suggest strongly on being cremated
    half of the ashes to be thrown to the wind
    if not at least a mild breeze and the remaining
    half to be smoked by a handful of friends in a
    chillum mixed with hashish of superior qualité
    and to spend a moment remembering some of the
    good things they shared with me

Tim Dlugos

NIGHT LIFE

for Ed Cox

The lives we lead at night:
you are on the streets of my
city, and I am asleep. In
my dream you are talking
to an old man, white beard.
You call him Fritz. You
call him Walt. It does not
matter what you call him;
he is just an old man.

You and he have made the same
choices. Now you think there's
something you should know. You
want him to tell you, but he
will not speak. You are both walking
down Spruce Street, and you are alone.

You are in denim. You are
in therapy, too. You learn
what you mean when you talk
out loud. Sometimes you learn
in your sleep. In strange cities,
we discover the way we can be.
We learn that we have always
been talking to ourselves. People
lead their lives all the time.

FAMOUS WRITERS

With famous writers you rarely know
what to expect. But sometimes
there are clues. The Maya in
Mayakovsky, for example, as in
"All is . . .". The secret Hem of
Hemingway. Closet writers give us
many clues. Those two blew
their skulls apart with gunshots.
Most famous writers have died, one way

or another. Frank O'Hara: the magnificent
OH in his name is what you say
when you're on the street pretending to be
Frank O'Hara. He may have said it himself
on the beach that night. And the Man
at the end of Berryman, which appears too
in Whitman, but means something different.

DAY LIGHT

for Bob

There are people, and there is
a man. His face cuts through our eyelids
like a smoky light. Whenever we speak
we are secretly talking to him.

I shall be able to write great books
when I see him, you will be
able to pay your bills. He will make us
woozy with his smoky love. When we are watching
each other we remember these things. We go home
alone or together, with wandering eyes.

There are kisses, and there is
a kiss. It lives among our rumors
like the family dog. We open our eyes
and it's day light, just as we expected.

Robert Duncan

THE TORSO

Most beautiful!   the red-flowering eucalyptus,
the madrone, the yew

Is he . . .

So thou wouldst smile, and take me in thine arms
The sight of London to my exiled eyes
Is as Elysium to a new-come soul

If he be Truth
I would dwell in the illusion of him

His hands unlocking from chambers of my male body

such an idea in man's image

rising tides that sweep me towards him

. . . homosexual?

and at the treasure of his mouth

pour forth my soul

his soul   commingling

I thought a Being more than vast, His body leading
into Paradise,   his eyes
quickening a fire in me,   a trembling

hieroglyph: At the root of the neck

the clavicle, for the neck is the stem of the great artery
upward into his head that is beautiful

At the rise of the pectoral muscles

the nipples, for the breasts are like sleeping fountains
of feeling in man, waiting above the beat of his heart,
shielding the rise and fall of his breath, to be

awakend

At the axis of his mid hriff

the navel, for in the pit of his stomach the chord from
which first he was fed has its temple

At the root of the groin

the pubic hair, for the torso is the stem in which the man
flowers forth and leads to the stamen of flesh in which
his seed rises

a wave of need and desire over   taking me

cried out my name

(This was long ago.   It was another life)

and said,

What do you want of me?

I do not know, I said.   I have fallen in love.   He
has brought me into heights and depths my heart
would fear   without him.   His look

pierces my side   •   fire eyes   •

I have been waiting for you, he said:
I know what you desire

you do not yet know   but through me   •

And I am with you everywhere.   In your falling

I have fallen from a high place.   I have raised myself

from darkness in your   rising

wherever you are

my hand in your hand   seeking   the locks, the keys

I am there.   Gathering me, you gather

your Self   •

For my Other is not a woman but a man

the King upon whose bosom let me lie.

might have been.
Certainly these ashes might have been pleasures.
Pilgrims on their way to the Holy Places remark
this place. Isn't it plain to all
that these mounds were palaces? This was once
a city among men, a gathering together of spirit.
It was measured by the Lord and found wanting.

It was measured by the Lord and found wanting,
destroyd by the angels that inhabit longing.
Surely this is Great Sodom where such cries
as if men were birds flying up from the swamp
ring in our ears, where such fears that were once
desires walk, almost spectacular,
stalking the desolate circles, red eyed.

This place rumord to have been a City surely was,
separated from us by the hand of the Lord.
The devout have laid out gardens in the desert,
drawn water from springs where the light was blighted.
How tenderly they must attend these friendships
or all is lost. All *is* lost.
Only the faithful hold this place green.

Only the faithful hold this place green
where the crown of fiery thorns descends.
Men that once lusted grow listless. A spirit
wrapped in a cloud, ashes more than ashes,
fire more than fire, ascends.
Only these new friends gather joyous here,
where the world like Great Sodom lies under fear.

The world like Great Sodom lies under Love
and knows not the hand of the Lord that moves.
This the friends teach where such cries
as if men were birds fly up from the crowds
gatherd and howling in the heat of the sun.
In the Lord Whom the friends have named at last Love
the images and loves of the friends never die.
This place rumord to have been Sodom is blessd
in the Lord's eyes.

David Eberly

From THE DELSARTE METHOD

unfolds
harmoniously,
an inflection of limbs,
rhythmic expression of distance,
a pushing away
or embrace
grace
sustained by strength,
                        that is,

1.
a flurry of hands: he stands
between bar stools
dreaming,
botticellian youth,
bound in blond smoke,
and buoyed up by scheming
weight over opposite leg leans
as if leaving.
              hearts
hook his belt and hold the fake greeting.

2.
in every gesture is the promised beginning,
however coy:
what fear signals alarm?
the boy masks surprise,
eyes and mouth open,
raised brow.
now:
the hand rounds toward the arm,

3.
flashing attraction.
his hand
                opens like a fan
(the heart of this motion.)
he presents
his palm to another man,

4.
developing emotion,
developing emotion.

SHORT LETTER

what can i say to you? nothing.
i nurture a sticky silence,
and turn to a simpler language.
i water my plants.

my life grows more solid without you.
i am concentric, a shell.
i wrap one word around another
until opaque, i rebuild a memory.

i watch my plants grow, adding cells.
how do they thrive on so little?
water and light. some days
i remember with pain.

dark of the moon. nothing
comes to fruition.
in the bars men
embrace,
their backs arching tight smiles.
the jukebox is too loud,
is laughter.
outside the trees are bare
and white, illuminated
by electric lights.
talking to myself i hear
other voices. eight months
i have not loved another.

POEM

i do not have nightmares.
i dream of urinals
rising from dead leaves and mud,
cool, white and graceful,
reflected in small pools.

i am not afraid.
i feel a warm wind on my face and on my hands.
my hands turn like brown leaves.
they lay themselves on the wet enamel.
they wait.

Jim Eggeling

THIRTEEN:

A
FIFTH FOR TH FOURTH
     AT
JIM'S.
_____

for Jim, of course

      i
   among th
PLANTS. PAINTINGS
BIEDERMEYER CHAIRS
   & th
Tilestove
   from
OSLO
   comes th
Longhaired & quite delicate
   little
   greatgreat
Grandson of ROBERT BRUCE
EXCLAIMING: : :
   O HOW
PRETTY! . . .
Bowing.
Smiling
Prancing & complaining
   because
HIS apartment isn't as pretty
ALSO.

   HOW
LOVELY TH BOY
   TH
FIREWORKS. HOW LOVELY.

                    ii
              OH HOW
        PRETTY TH TADASKI:
                    th
        Crystal from which I drink my whiskey.
                    the original
        Colville & th Picasso
                    near th
        Windowsill.
                    th pet
        Cat.
                    th
        Carpets & stoney hearth . . .
                    . . . th
        REAL WOOD table.
                    th
        Silver & candles
                    &
        Cushiondeep divan
                    in which you
        Lie.
        Experimentally disabled
                    (for 1
        Minute.)

              HOW
        LOVELY TH SPARKLER
              TH
        ROCKET. HOW LOVELY

                    iii
              HOW
        PRETTY TH VIEW OF TH CITY
                    Jim's
        Balconyview of th pines
                    &
        Twilight crowds of peoples . . .
              HAPPY
        FOURTH OF JULY:
                    you
        shout down eight floors.

Ignoring
Houston
Highrise
Mores.

iv
HOW
LOVELY LITTLE RUSSEL
AS
LOVELY AS TH SPARKS
TO WHICH HE
SHOUTS:
HOW
PRETTY!
Rockets
Break th sky.
th
Sparks fall dizzily
Bloody.
Verdant.
Sizzling on th grass
to
Die.

v
th
Boy's gone out
th
Punk is gutted
GOODNIGHT LITTLE RUSSEL.
GOODNIGHT.
TONIGHT YOU WERE THIRTEEN.
Next
YEAR.
YOU'LL BE
THIRTY.
GOODNIGHT LOVELY BOY.
(YOU
TOO. OLD MAN.)
(*HOW*
PRETTY!)

CHAN EX

for Rudy

Son of Kukulcan:
       yr
Flesh is dark as choc'late.
Sweet . . .
Candy for th Jaguargod.
Roaring in th rain of Copan . . .
Slinking through th street.

Boy of delicate Mayas:
Love me. loving
        you.
Boy with coral fingers.
Touch me. touching
        you . . . yr
Beauty is my song.
Singing you. my song
        is
Soft with yr breath.

        (little
Brother: breathe my kisses.
        little
Brother breathe my breath.)

Child of Kukulcan:
        lisp
Rain to cool my heat.
Boy with th jade ring . . .
        let me
Drink near yr pillow
        th
Feathers of yr liquid breath.
        yr
Flesh as sweet as choc'late . . .
Candy for th Jaguargod . . .
Slinking through th street.

INVOCATION

Littleboys. underground / river of / HOMOSEXUALITY
Sucking each other by matchlight/ in / Blackbowled caverns
                        Littleboys in denims
                        Baseball
                                caps . . .
                        Balling
                                one another behind broken
                        Backstops
Littleboys. naked / Rolling in th stickers . . .
Littleboys courting th most ENORMOUS/ of/ Bigboys' thornes
                        Littleboys. clothed.
                                their little
                        Penises, wobbling
                                up out of their
                        Juvenile flies . . .
                        Delinquents in behalf of LOVE

Breaking th law in innocence / Believing in sex:
Writing it on walls . . .
LITTLEBOYS COME!

Quivering with pleasure. / Hiding it in toilets:
Sucking th OLDMEN . . .
LITTLEBOYS COME!

Yelling from treehouse / to / Treehouse. then sucking
        each others'
Boyhood tasting manhood . . .
LITTLEBOYS COME!

COME IN TH TREEHOUSE!
                (Yelling into th sky)
COME IN TH CAVERN!
                (Burning into th damp)

                                out of th
                        Ground like artesian water
                                out of th
                        Forest

```
                    under
            Snow.
            LITTLEBOYS COME!
Come in each other / Rivers that mingle . . .
        like artesian
Springs
        their little
PENISES
COME!

LITTLEBOYS. those underground rivers / of /
                    HOMOSEXUALITY.  COME!
```

Drawing by Wilton David (gleep)

Kenward Elmslie

APRIL 2: THE WALTZ

They were conversing in a lisping tone of voice.

"Hotel Chelsea, wonderful place to be alone. Big room. A kid, fiddling with himself, Shanty-Irish, red-headed, 16 or 17. Why don't I like kids? Feeling me. Why no reaction? He looks scared."

When they drank, they extended their pinkies in a very dainty manner.

"I don't live far from here. Gotta get back home."

They took short sips from their straws. They were very very endearing to one another, very delicate to each other.

"Damn thing starts, smell it coming. Take nap. He runs back, jumps on bed, lies there. Tremble and shake. Stays. Tie him up. That's the war. Over the edge blindness. Come. Sick. Untie him. Go away. Likes that. Comes back once. Stupid gift. Doesn't want to be any different. Comes to town once or twice a month. Can't hurt him—he likes it. Ice all over. Licks. Untie him. Goes away. Don't you ever come, baby? Ice all over me. Snow. Gunfire. Part of me likes it. White fog."

It took a long time to finish their drinks. When walking, getting up from the stools, they very politely excused each other, holding onto the arm.

LEND-A-HAND HAIKU

Wave blue checkbook at black lashes
on profile over sink, Etruscan doe-eyed steal-a-heart youth?
Nope. Just watch him wash the dishes.

My Army   likes you so much. The young cadets
in their handsome yellow boots
and kepis and sashes . . .

My Army   how to explain, my very own Army,
the orderlies, the nurses, the countermen,
the laundresses, their new silence?

My Army   loves you, I think. Whether they be pursers
mechanics, eye doctors, night watchmen,
those iron-faced officers . . .

My Army   feels sick today. The men are all grumbling,
they want to join your side—you!—and then
celebrate victory with fireworks and parades.
They request a photo of your singing voice
for the imminent fireworks and parades.
Candids of you are welcome in case of
fireworks and parades, as are any movies
of you yourself chewing smiling etc.
even sleeping etc. for the about-to-commence
fireworks and parades.

* * * * * * *

*'His whole army is infatuated, infatuated.
A silly god rose out of the sea, made out
of sexy tin with bandages here and there
and it makes hitherto unheard-of sounds,
and changes into man, woman, God, money,
disease, social justice, Beauty—at will!
Benjamin Franklin has a sick headache.
O where is the country heading, and what
can I, a mere man, do?'*
     —*George Washington*

* * * * * * *

My Army   likes you so much. The young cadets
in their handsome yellow boots
and kepis and sashes

call you obscenities softly. Dedicated?
There is no raillery in the latrines,
and in their sleep they moan
Fuck me suck me fuck me suck me

My Army   loves you I think. At strategy conferences
those iron-faced officers thrash out
memories of your tinniest sounds.
Tears fall on crucial mountains.
Dilemmas of survival . . .

* * * * * * *

'*I hear the sound of mandolins. Let me
fly away with you.*'
                                   —*Theodore Roosevelt*

* * * * * * *

My Army   keeps busy.
Man 20 feet. Man 20 feet. Man 20 feet.
Guarding pipelines from desert area to
industrial complex.
Testing sirens, scrubbing sirens, painting
sirens,
guarding the oils and gases necessary
for the siren system, and so the years
pass and pass.

My Army   likes you so much.
If state secrets arrive
(in food, lightbulbs, street refuse)
thank the spies.
Who vie with each other for blueprints.
Who envy the corridor-like structure
of your chicaneries.
Who despise all who can hear your voice
in the threshing machines,
the mid-day boiler explosions,
the violin rallies.

* * * * * * *

*'An enemy trick rose out of the sea,
and his whole army went swimming.
Phooey. Bronze somersaults. Tonight
they returned in silence. Hellish bivouac,
blast the tom-toms. Meanwhile the animals
thump and wheeze, circling around our tiny
encampment, and the birds with their red
beaks screech and screech, and I wonder
how long can I keep the capitol inviolate?'*
                                    —*Douglas MacArthur*

* * * * * * *

My Army   loves you I think.
                But for fun it takes bus expeditions
                through the colossal Ice Zoo.
                Perfectly preserved, two black pumas
                locked in mortal combat. Two penguins
                locked in mortal combat. Perfectly preserved
                monkeys and birds, long extinct species,
                perfectly preserved, each in its own ice segment,
                locked in mortal combat, perfectly preserved.
                O dirty bus windows, let them see out.

My Army   sends you this historic painting
                Painting of You . . .
                BOOM!

My Army   likes you so much
                loves you I think so much
                they are marching to your hit recording *Me!*
                Hurry, when will *Us* be released?
                Panic is spreading, what will it sound like?
                A bleep, a sobby kid, two whole peoples?
                How to know, how to know.
                Hurry, is it smashed,
                help, where is it? Help!
                They my army wants to shout
                hello into your navel
                (Help!) and hear that old song
                (Help!) come out to explain
                (Help!) the seasons

(Help!) harvests
(Help!) plus certain facts about storms that start
(Help!) (Help!) on the (They can kill!)
moon.

APRIL 7: SICK BAY

Lying alone has been a precious time, because much has been relived, more and more am conscious of almost a new person inside (no, Maggie darling, I'm not turning sex-change on you) —something's in the atmosphere . . . a change in the weather . . . many of the men who've come back from Nam feel it very strongly, talk about it confusedly, reaching forwards. There's a violent time coming, and I suppose it's nature preparing her lovers against the violent men by some inner law that can't be analyzed yet, since it's just happening. Nothing to do with mysticism. Just a different emotional set-up. For instance, in the bed next to mine is a twenty-one year old. He comes from North Carolina of moneyed people. He described a trip down to his father's yacht in Palm Beach:

> I drove down to my father's boat with someone called Frank Frost: tallish, good-looking, golden blond, well built. He had a stubby clown nose and a Jack O'Lantern grin. I'd seen him only four times before our trip, only twice to talk to alone, once or twice, actually once, just once. Not alone exactly, we'd gone to the movies with two girl-friends of Frank's. They'd gone to powder their noses, and while we were standing by the refreshment counter, Frank asked me to share an apartment with him in New York after Summer School. Anyway, the day of the trip, we met early. We drank beer before breakfast. He was all in white. I could hardly look at him. We read *Reflections in a Golden Eye*. He thought the people were morbid. We got drunk, drove fast, 70 or 80—wild rushing through darkness. He was

asleep in the back seat. In Daytona Beach, I went to see a classmate of mine, Fred Beyer, marry Janice. I met her relatives: dim people, suffocating. They talked about presents and that's all. I drove a sixteen year-old girl home. She invited me in. We played records. She was very sweet. She played record after record, waiting to be kissed. I kissed her awkwardly, trying to be nice. I drove back to the hotel. Frank was still awake. After lights out, I said, *I'm cold.* I moved and lay beside him. After a moment he got angry. First puzzled, then angry. He said: *are you kidding. Fuck you.* I said: *but I'm cold.* He said: *don't stay here.* I said: *can't you sleep with me here?* He said: *no.* I went back to my bed and pretended to sleep. Next morning I asked him to walk to the beach with me, I had something very important to tell him. We walked on the beach and the silence grew longer and I tried to tell him, but I couldn't break it with words. I couldn't say a thing. My fumblings were—just peculiar to him, I guess. We left that afternoon after the wedding. The wedding was like a toy thing, with bright costumes, everything done accurately including rice pelting the car. Frank was impatient to get away. We stayed in my father's house in Palm Beach. My father liked Frank: *handsome* intelligent lad.

I don't want to leave here and resume my life. Food, sleep, the days float by—chess after dinner, then talk. Something's in the atmosphere though—a violent time is coming. Nothing to do with mysticism, just a different emotional set-up. These days, I don't seem to surface very often.

R. Daniel Evans

LETTER TO WALT WHITMAN

1.
Sometimes, when I'm at the beach I see your muse.
He's tall, goodlooking, has dark blond hair
and a bulge in the crotch of his blue bikini.
I'm sure you would have enjoyed running
your hand up his thigh or rubbing the sand
out of that longish blond hair, Old Walt.
He'd understand a lot of your poems, be a camerado,
and might start wearing a golden calamus root
on the same chain with his lambda sign.
It's terribly hard to work, Walt, when he's around.
Perspiration just rolls down my chest, when he's on
the beach, and not simply because it's 94 in the shade.
Don't know how you ever got your work done,
but bet you had a lot of fun.

2.
Walt, it's time for you
to send out the poets to the heartland,
tell them to eat corn on the cob,
throw quarters across the waves
at the Delaware River Water Gap (like George),
walk under the Brooklyn Bridge at night the way Hart Crane did,
paint a Maine in bright colors country of Marsden Hartley,
and stare down the throat of the Continental Divide in
Colorado like a hummingbird looking in the vagina of a hibiscus;
tell them to go grope some Grand Teton lumberjack
and sing with the wolves and coyotes a song of Jack London,
fish for giant Marlins in the Caribbean with a beard grown for
                    the occasion like Papa Hemingway's,
sip mint juleps and talk to magnolia belles with honey-voiced
                                        Tennessee,
cheerfully drink water from skulls & cacti alike in Death Valley,

wrestle with our Indian brothers who built Louis Sullivan's Chicago,
shoot up and wail blues with the black brothers in New Orleans
                                                    & Harlem,
recover spirits and minds on peyote buds in New Mexico,
and having done this and all these other American customs,
will be able to fill lines rich and ready like reeds with music,
harmonize the old & dying words,
give a boost to all the minorities
including all your sisters from Alaska to Hawaii
and your own minority, your gay brothers and sisters.

And help us, Walt, dream our dreams
torn from America's underside
polarized America, America in trouble, and let's
lay low delayed Victory, that tart & scrawny bitch
& let's have America speak through us:
Old Walt let's offer a
poem together
to the twenty-first century.

EYE PRAISE

I love your eyes;
in my dreams
my breath is on your pants
fluctuating seashell
my hand is on the zipper
starfish opening a shell
my hand petting your jock
blue sun warming a salty ocean.

I wake up to be drowned by
the sight of your naked back
shoulder blades the arched wings
of a compassionate eagle
who will not let me show pity as
I indulge in firm fleshed pain
the muscles of your back a map to my fingers
my eyes watched by your laughing eyes.

Gerald L. Fabian

AN ELEGY FOR A LOST SHIPMATE

I. *Prelude*
Underway, the dreadnought Queen that winter night
    we first stood mid-watch together on the
    portside flag bridge.
Top-heavy from too much armament when she rolled
    her foremast yard arm whooshed dizzily
    toward the white caps & swells.

Clang! went the buoy.

It grew darker as the moon and stars all disappeared,
    a cold black edge ripped our pea-coats,
    our inner warmth mounted.
I don't remember where—Hampton Roads, off
    Cape Charles . . . passing stormy Hatteras.
Our conversation gone, but not our tropism—
    only remains your flaxen hair which threw
    off a suffused glow, replacing the absent
    heavens.
As two ephebes trying to become men we absolutely
    did not embrace, or did we?

When I gently drew up your collar to protect
    your stinging ears.

II.
AN ELEGY FOR A LOST SHIMATE, A BUCKEYE
    HYACINTHUS, IN WHICH THE QUOIT
        MISSES HIS TEMPLE, BUT
        STRIKES HIS CONSCIOUSNESS.

III.
Your strangely rough and chapped skin; your powerful,
    even curiously horny hands, like those of a farm
    boy instead of city-bred from Cleveland, or was
    it Amyclae?

Hardness from work in the fields, or premature aging
    from the poverty of the thirties, and underneath,
    unsuspected, lingered a virginal child who somehow
    bespoke gothic riches of old monasteries.

IV.
Androgynous ambiguity driving some of the crew to
    despair with desire for your impossibly
    small waist, [dancer on a frieze at the
    Palace of Knossos], the moulding of your
    pectorals—"morphodite" apples too large
    for a boy, full snowy lilies in baroque
    paintings capped by nipples, small roseate
    floribunda.

I can't describe your other splendors, like a
    Tuscan farmer of the quattrocento according
    to Merezhkovsky, whose plough had just
    struck the marble of a *kouros,* I was too
    awestruck & superstitious to look!

All the luminescence of your pale form:
    In the fan-tail shower room you had to
    accept a rain of innuendo that frequently
    goaded you to a mute anger.

Salvatore Farinella

JULY 4TH THREESOME

Sperm smeared across your back
we lie breathlessly side by side;
the sliding over sweat
slipping bodies momentarily over.
There are the drugs we drag into our lungs,
short snort into our heads and then the lunge
into each other's arms. Warmth
as we sink into undulations
the waves the ocean throws away
from herself—O Moma—the music radio
batons the head, the heart
beats its foot to it and I
surf boarding over you new two lovers'
chests find myself impaled
and how to move with it
this breathing the ocean, this water
dripping from us glistening
droplets from the ends of our eyebrows, our noses
those taps turned with two passing lovers'
hands that speak of water free
to reminisce of trumpets at dusk;
a funeral, a river from the sky,
makes its way to the horizon.

TONIGHT

Tomorrow his eyes will be open,
alert after the swim
and filled with sensual glistening bodies:
youthful   angular
males energetically splashing;
mist falling on his lips.

At the tone the time
will be eleven o'clock and fifty seconds.

Defying gravity smoke
slowly from his nose   past his lidded eyes
in other worldly wanderings
tomorrow the perfect
day: loose like a winter scarf in spring
(slowly from his nose   past his lidded eyes)
the crowded street bares its youth.

At the tone the time will be
eleven o'clock and fifty five seconds.

Sensuality will pull at his lower lip
with stranger's teeth   the enticement,
the pleasure of sharing youth's
careless beauty   the teeth
in the darkened cubicle
nipping at his skin tomorrow
where his firm body will be male
(At the tone the time will be twelve o'clock exactly)

will satiate my lust for them
and keep my sharing my bed with him tonight.

EPITHALAMION

Undressing (you in the locker room)
between metal doors I noticed
(as I passed) out the corner of my eye
but instantly forgot in a flurry of bodies
then in that darkness
spinning mirror scales all the light
you sat near timid at the edge
of the forest meadow. You do not know
me hunted and yet hunter but we
touch toe, ankle, calf, knee thigh
fold and know together talk won't get us there.
How my fright alerted me you
were he growing up a few steps behind;
the child I loved and continue to love
afar even now your wedding taking place.
The bride how beautiful! and fawning guests
fanning themselves with starched silken fans.
No one talks about the groom
his beautiful wrists, the hairs which ornament
that miniature forest of tree tops bending
slightly with wind sluggish in summer.
You are the July groom beauty
no rose named for you.
That room of dizzy lights
could be anywhere yet in San Francisco
both of us men making love
didn't dare talk for fear recognition
in this city of fantasy comes true.

[untitled]

I haven't heard a sound for days
Like an Indian snake
my cock rises and faces me.

DEAD END ORGY

Floating at the end of the blow job
anonymous suck in the dark, tangled labyrinth
my fingers anchored in hair,
I sight you my white ghost lover
sail across darkness
to cascade over the body
next to me   unaware of me.

(In the darkness of our bed
you gave me the deep fall
into your body, my fascination
rivets your infidelity.)

You phosphorescent satellite
can not pull away. Turning
(do you know I'm here?)
you slide onto the stranger's sex
and I glide off
luminous in artificial night
looking for two strong hands.

NEW EACH TIME

Curious in the cave of your body
wide-eyed animal blood
lifts my sex stick
a spitting sparkler on the 4th of July.

THE EXPERIENCE

Walking past the meat rack
along the river, across
the Japanese bridge
to the other side, I played
a game of Lock Eyes
with strangers in black
coats, short coats, fur coats;
kept on walking
until I was alone
with snow and ice.

In soft white, I scratched:

Unlike you,
Cavafy,
I can not thank
the experience
for having exceeded the previous one.

WINTER KILL

How odd. This stranger walks
beside me talking
carelessly about bitter
cold. We will enter dark
places where even rats have left
and make quick love
Over—he will run
away as though he
sucked on a leper's body.

Edward Field

THE MOVING MAN

He was a burly, curly-blond ape of a man
who had a moving van
and a bunch of young helpers he paid by the job.
He treated those boys like a harem,
picking one for his pleasure when he wanted.
He had wrestled them all to defeat
for when they fell under his weight
with that huge body on them
they went dreamy as desire took them
and they let it.

Having him for example, they were a rowdy gang
hanging around the office at the front of the garage
waiting for a job to be called in,
always wrestling and grabbing at each other
with an eye cocked for the boss's approval,
half-teasing him with their slim bodies
muscled from the work.
The van stood behind in the shadows
with its tailgate down, empty
except for the quilts used to wrap furniture in,
lying in a heap.

In the idleness of the afternoon
the boss would start horsing around with a boy,
perhaps one who had been especially fresh,
and chasing him through the dark garage
force him right up the tailgate into the van.
There they fell rolling on the quilts
until the man, pinning him with his chest,
pulled down the boy's pants—
his own were always open.
His large hand roved down the naked belly

to the clutch of hair and hard-standing prick—
with balls, a handful—
and the boy yelped, but had to stay.

His wrestler arms tamed that young body like an animal:
Holding him prisoner, he forced him over,
his cock probing the backs of his thighs,
the cheeks of his ass,
thrusting all over to find the moist center.
One hand on a breast fingered the nipple,
the other arm pulled him closer below
to the hot push, demanding entrance.
His mouth bit at the boy's neck,
breathed hard on the plum of a cheek,
his stubble scratching as he growled in the boy's ear,
teaching him pleasure.

Now he held in his arms the whole boy
his fat prick pushed between those round cheeks,
until the boy, completely submerged in that loving hulk of a man,
relaxed with a moan and opened
and the moving man moved his prick all the way in,
taking his time.

STREET INSTRUCTIONS: AT THE CROTCH

> *It is not against the law to grope yourself.*
> —D.D.T.
> *Remember yourself.*
> —Gurdjieff

While walking toward housewife wheeling baby
reach down and squeeze your cock,
looking at her casually.

Adjust cock from left side to right
causing half hard-on,
then shift it back.

Wear balls on one side, cock on other.

Tug at crotch of pants as if to free genitals
tangled in underwear.
Give it a good tugging.
Go out without underwear.

Make small tear in bulge of basket
exposing skin.
Sew patch on crudely.

Wear pants of some material
flimsy as the law allows.

Go out with fly unzippered.
Go out with fly half unbuttoned.
Break zipper and fasten with safety pin.
Rip crotch and sew with large jagged stitches.

While talking with friends
unzip fly, lower pants, and arrange shirt tails.

Ask policeman for directions
and while he's telling you
give yourself a feel.

Walk loosely
to give yourself as much stimulation as you can.
Let it all move.
Be there.

Charles Henri Ford

THEIR IMAGES I LOVED I VIEW IN THEE

Skinning back the living teeth of Asia
It will rain all night he said
My love may not be pure but it is complete
And poetry is a lyric wisdom or it doesn't last
A quiet dawn and sleep in the body says, 'What have you done
            to me?'
". . . activity without attachment" —poetry a form of Buddhism,
            Buddhism a form of poetry

The suns burn through and Kathmandu will burn into your heart
Heavy showers keep lovers with nacreous masks trapped in their
            mansions
". . . it's forever the same murmur, flowing unbroken like a
            single endless word and therefore meaningless"
Yes, he's the beloved. And I aspire to his favors. Do I wish
            he were a woman? No!
"The tangled net of ruin/ Which passion casts . . ."
With houses as with people, you love them you use them you
            leave them
Who belongs most to what

Writing comes out like a perfume to attract no one there is
            no one to attract
Sway, banana leaf, I too am swaying I know how you feel
Living as though we had all the time in the world—and we had;
            and we have

> "... the death, then, of a beautiful woman
> is, unquestionably, the most poetical topic
> in the world ..."
> —Poe

The King of the Monkeys tried to marry her
As though he had not been upset enough in his life she was eager
        to upset him more
From the nursery of murderers he led you to the golden dustheap
Entering a supersensual universe spun by the human spider
You stood by a window that framed the dogwood, just to prove the
        folly of a diamond-tipped knife
I saw the fiendish treatment you gave to a young pearl
To identify the opposites of an artificial order a dwarf was
        sewn to your abdomen with secret threads
Bereft of origin and change wrapped in wire cloth white hard but
        malleable they buried you in the skin of a
        black deer
To small heartless caterpillars you are the sorcerer-saint
        dissolving in star-showers
Exquisite aberration, the garment of decay was not for you
Like an upside-down butterfly or a man without eyebrows in all
        that rushing annihilation yours was the historic
        aura of a peacock's grace
You went as a stranger where strangers go, broken crescent in a
        sky of enigmas
Moonlit birds have alighted holding a rosary of human teeth in
        claws of bright benevolent steel
I lift the glass of veneration to a glimmering vision, explosive
        flower planted in the mud of a lawless world

Paris is waiting with open arms and pissoirs
Dr. Thapa stressed the need
For teaching beggars how to face the ups and downs of life
And the clock-makers have donated a clock for the bell tower
Category of false needs, red on rubbing, black-red on
            rubbing, multi-sensuous
After wrecking the Garden of Eden the revolutionaries regained
            their bases safely
They are swatting flies with the face of Nixon on an old copy
            of Newsweek
Lady Luck's a nymphomaniac silver white green on green
Love tension (and what is love but tension)
Will never relax as long as she imposes
The yoke of retention
A sugar factory in Kenya
Will now produce ballistic missiles to comb away the dew
Name two kinds of fever comet fever swine fever
Boy with violin serenades ruined folly of swollen city
The tradition of hidden sayings deciphered in meteoric streams
'I'm only poetry, soul, nothing else' (Mayakovsky)
You're nobody until it's all outside of you for everybody to see
You strike an attitude, you camp, nothing is real but your love
And a fact of bitch life is, that when you have sex appeal you
            can't keep it just for yourself
Master of your style, that's all you have to be, let who will be
            master of your fate
But when time stands still that's when we hate it most
The air blue as hemorrhoids
Sometimes my genius is too much for me but not often
And so we partake of the vitality of the damned
Like kangaroo rats with perennial roots and primordial germ cells
The embryo's future head is in the absent scrotum of the skeleton

Clue to the forgetful hogfest, as told to our slob in
      Tangier. A purse-snatching horse-breeder, re-
      nowned for Anna May Wong charme et beauté,
      spreads his scrotal sac (white supremacy where
      it really hurts).
No one can revile with a plastic heart. In a formal
      dinner jacket every doctor would look like Gore
      Vidal (author of "Myra Breckenridge") at a loss
      for words. Please pass the mixed media arms
      race cartridge.
Gregory Corso, who hung a trompe-l'oeil curse in my
      mouth, substitutes meaning for the teachings
      of a cross-eyed sexpot.
That's the genius of the Great Ritual. "It's competi-
      tive!" A popular expression meaning heaven on
      earth.
But Shelley, seeing what he wanted to see (intercom
      thralldom) had the look and feel of a turned-on
      co-pilot.
The instructions are to fling it to Miss Mentholatum.
Nor could snatch impersonation have created a
      distress signal, Burroughs says. A 12-year-old cock looks
      lovely by candlelight. In the background,
      portrait of an electric toothbrush.

James Giancarlo

ANGELS OF LIGHT

You call yourselves
Angels of Light: lunar
sideshow;
sons of suns;
light of the fire
that burns to be seen
and sanctify

hard sparkle plenty
and shine

Tinsel wings spread
open in the spotlight;
boycocks bounce
beneath taffeta flounces
& fringe, poke
sequined foreskins
through lavender lace
into Androgyny
to show us our bodies
are arbitrary
and often lie.

We watch from the darkness
of our audience disguise
scream
OutRageUs!
from our small masquerades.

[Ed. Note: The Angels of Light are an anarchistic gender fuck
theatre group in San Francisco.]

Allen Ginsberg

NIGHT GLEAM

Over and over thru the dull material world the call is made
over and over thru the dull material world I make the call
O English folk, in Sussex night, thru black beech tree branches
the full moon shone at three AM, I stood in under wear on the
    lawn—
I saw a mustached English man I loved, athlete's breast and
    farmer's arms,
I lay in bed that night many loves beating in my heart
sleepless hearing songs of generations returning intelligent
    memory
to my frame, and so went to dwell again in my heart
and worship the Lovers there, love's teachers, youths and poets
    who live forever
in the secret heart, in the dark night, in the full moon, year after
    year
over & over thru the dull material world the call is made.

11 July 1973

CHANCES "R"

Nymph and shepherd raise electric tridents
      glowing red against the plaster wall,
The jukebox beating out magic syllables,
A line of painted boys snapping fingers
        & shaking thin Italian trouserlegs
            or rough dungarees on big asses
                bumping and dipping
ritually, with no religion but the
            old one of cocksuckers
naturally, in Kansas center of America
        the farmboys in Diabolic bar light
      alone stiff necked or lined up
      dancing row on row like Afric husbands
& the music's sad here, whereas Sunset Trip or
Jukebox Corner it's ecstatic pinball machines—
Religiously, with concentration and free
            prayer; fairy boys of the plains
            and their gay sisters of the city
step together to the center of the floor
        illumined by machine eyes, screaming drumbeats,
            passionate voices of Oklahoma City
                chanting No Satisfaction
Suspended from Heaven the Chances R
      Club floats rayed by stars
        along a Wichita tree avenue
        traversed with streetlights on the plain.

February 1966

PLEASE MASTER

Please master can I touch your cheek
please master can I kneel at your feet
please master can I loosen your blue pants
please master can I gaze at your golden haired belly
please master can I gently take down your shorts
please master can I have your thighs bare to my eyes
please master can I take off my clothes below your chair
please master can I kiss your ankles and soul
please master can I touch lips to your hard muscle hairless thigh
please master can I lay my ear pressed to your stomach
please master can I wrap my arms around your white ass
please master can I lick your groin curled with blond soft fur
please master can I touch my tongue to your rosy asshole
please master may I pass my face to your balls,
please master, please look into my eyes,
please master order me down on the floor
please master tell me to lick your thick shaft
please master put your rough hands on my bald hairy skull
please master press my mouth to your prick-heart
please master press my face into your belly, pull me slowly
          strong thumbed
till your dumb hardness fills my throat to the base
till I swallow & taste your delicate flesh-hot prick barrel veined
          Please
Master push my shoulders away and stare in my eye, & make
          me bend over the table
please master grab my thighs and lift my ass to your waist
please master your hand's rough stroke on my neck your palm
          down my backside
please master push me up, my feet on chairs, till my hole feels
          the breath of your spit and your thumb stroke
please master make me say Please Master Fuck me now Please
Master grease my balls and hairmouth with sweet vaselines
please master stroke your shaft with white creams
please master touch your cock head to my wrinkled self-hole
please master push it in gently, your elbows enwrapped round
          my breast

your arms passing down to my belly, my penis you touch w/your
        fingers
please master shove it in me a little, a little, a little,
please master sink your droor thing down my behind
& please master make me wiggle my rear to eat up the prick
        trunk
till my asshalfs cuddle your thighs, my back bent over,
till I'm alone sticking out, your sword stuck throbbing in me
please master pull out and slowly roll into the bottom
please master lunge it again, and withdraw to the tip
please please master fuck me again with your self, please fuck
        me Please
Master drive down till it hurts me the softness the
Softness please master make love to my ass, give body to center,
        & fuck me for good like a girl,
tenderly clasp me please master I take me to thee,
& drive in my belly your selfsame sweet heat-rood
you fingered in solitude Denver or Brooklyn or fucked in a
        maiden in Paris carlots
please master drive me thy vehicle, body of love drops, sweat
        fuck
body of tenderness, Give me your dog fuck faster
please master make me go moan on the table
Go moan O please master do fuck me like that
in your rhythm thrill-plunge & pull-back-bounce & push down
till I loosen my asshole a dog on the table yelping with terror
        delight to be loved
Please master call me a dog, an ass beast, a wet asshole,
& fuck me more violent, my eyes hid with your palms round my
        skull
& plunge down in a brutal hard lash thru soft drip-flesh
& throb thru five seconds to spurt out your semen heat
over & over, bamming it in while I cry out your name I do love
        you
please Master.

May 1968

ON NEAL'S ASHES

Delicate eyes that blinked blue Rockies all ash
nipples, Ribs I touched w/ my thumb are ash
mouth my tongue touched once or twice all ash
bony cheeks soft on my belly are cinder, ash
earlobes & eyelids, youthful cock tip, curly pubis
breast warmth, man palm, high school thigh,
baseball bicept arm, asshole anneal'd to silken skin
all ashes, all ashes again.

August 1968

MESSAGE

Since we had changed
rogered spun worked
wept and pissed together
I wake up in the morning
with a dream in my eyes
but you are gone in NY
remembering me Good
I love you I love you
& your brothers are crazy
I accept their drunk cases
It's too long that I have been alone
it's too long that I've sat up in bed
without anyone to touch on the knee, man
or woman I don't care what anymore, I
want love I was born for I want you with me now
Ocean liners boiling over the Atlantic
Delicate steelwork of unfinished skyscrapers
Back end of the dirigible roaring over Lakehurst
Six women dancing together on a red stage naked

The leaves are green on all the trees in Paris now
I will be home in two months and look you in the eyes

1958

MESSAGE II

Long since the years
letters songs Mantras
eyes apartments bellies
kissed and grey bridges
walked across in mist
Now your brother's Welfare's
paid by State now Lafcadio's
home with Mama, now you're
in NY beds with big poetic
girls & go picket on the street
I clang my finger-cymbals in Havana, I lie
with teenage boys afraid of the red police,
I jack off in Cuban modern bathrooms, I ascend
over blue oceans in a jet plane, the mist hides
the black synagogue, I will look for the Golem,
I hide under the clock near my hotel, its intermission
for Tales of Hoffman, nostalgia for the 19th century
rides through my heart like the music of Die Moldau,
I'm still alone with long black beard and shining eyes
walking down black smokey tramcar streets at night
past royal muscular statues on an old stone bridge,
Over the river again today in Breughel's wintery city,
the snow is white on all the rooftops of Prague,
Salute beloved comrade I'll send you my tears from Moscow.

March 1965

CITY MIDNIGHT JUNK STRAINS

for Frank O'Hara

Switch on lights yellow as the sun
                          in the bedroom . . .
The gaudy poet dead   Frank O'Hara's bones
                          under cemetery grass
An emptiness at 8PM in the Cedar Bar
        Throngs of drunken
                  guys talking about paint
        & lofts, and Pennsylvania youth.
                  Kline attacked by his heart
& chattering Frank
                  stopped forever—
        Faithful drunken adorers, mourn.
                  The busfare's a nickle more
        past his old apartment 9th Street by the park.
Delicate Peter loved his praise,
        I wait for the things he says
                          about me—
        Did he think me an Angel
        as angel I am still talking into earth's microphone
                          willy nilly
        —to come back as words ghostly hued
                          by early death
        but written so bodied
                  mature in another decade.
Chatty prophet
                  of yr own loves, personal
                  memory feeling fellow
        Poet of building-glass
I see you walking you said with your tie
        flopped over your shoulder   in the wind down 5th Ave
                under the handsome breasted workmen
                        on their scaffolds ascending Time
                          & washing the windows of Life
—off to a date with Martinis & a blond
                beloved poet far from home
                —with thee and Thy sacred Metropolis

in the enormous bliss   of a long afternoon
where death is the shadow
            cast by Rockefeller Center
                over your intimate street.
Who were you, black suited, hurrying to meet,
        Unsatisfied one?
                Unmistakable,
                        Darling date
for the charming solitary   young poet with a big cock
                who could fuck you all night long
                    till you never came,
        trying your torture on his   obliging fond body
        eager to satisfy god's whim that made you
                Innocent,   as you are.
I tried   your boys and found them ready
        sweet and amiable
            collected gentlemen
                with large sofa apartments
        lonesome to please   for pure language;
and you mixed with money
                because you knew enough language to be rich
                    if you wanted your walls to be empty—
Deep philosophical terms dear Edwin Denby serious as Herbert
        Read
        with silvery hair   announcing your dead gift
to the grave crowd   whose historic op art   frisson was
the new sculpture your big blue wounded body made in the
                                Universe
        when you went away   to Fire Island for the weekend
    tipsy with a family of decade-olden friends

Peter stares out the window   at robbers
        the Lower East Side   distracted in Amphetamine
I stare into my head   & look for your / broken roman nose
        your wet mouth-smell of martinis
                & a big artistic tipsy kiss.
    40's only half a life   to have filled
            with so many fine parties and evenings'
        interesting drinks together with one
                    faded friend or new
                    understanding social cat . . .

I want to be there in your garden party in the clouds
                        all of us naked
strumming our harps and reading each other   new poetry
            in the boring celestial
                        friendship Committee Museum.
You're in a bad mood?
                        Take an Asprin.
                        In the Dumps?
                            I'm falling asleep
                                safe in your thoughtful arms.
Someone uncontrolled by History would have to own Heaven,
                                on earth as it is.
I hope you satisfied your childhood love
        Your puberty fantasy   your sailor punishment on your knees
                            your mouth-suck
Elegant insistency
                    on the honking self-prophetic Personal
                    as Curator of funny emotions to the mob,
Trembling One, whenever possible. I see New York thru your eyes
            and hear of one funeral a year nowadays—
                        From Billie Holiday's time
                    appreciated more and more
a common ear
                        for our deep gossip.

July 29, 1966

John Giorno

PORNOGRAPHIC POEM

Seven Cuban
army officers
in exile
were at me
all night.
Tall,
sleek,
slender
Spanish types
with smooth dark
muscular bodies
and hair
like wet coal
on their heads
and between their legs.
I lost count
of the times
I was fucked
by them
in every conceivable
position.
At one point
they stood
around me
in a circle
and I had
to crawl
from one crotch
to another
sucking
on each cock
until it was hard.

When I got all
seven up
I shivered
looking up
at those erect pricks
all different lengths
and widths
and knowing
that each one
was going up
my ass hole.
Everyone
of them
came
at least twice
and some three times.
Once they put me
on the bed
kneeling,
one fucked me
in the behind,
another in the mouth,
while I jacked off
one
with each hand
and two
of the others
rubbed
their peckers
on my bare feet
waiting
their turns
to get
into my can.
Just when I thought
they were all spent
two of them
got together
and fucked me
at once.

The positions
we were in
were crazy
but with two
big fat
Cuban cocks
up my ass
at one time
I was
in paradise.

[*Untitled*]

I reached
under
his waist
I reached under his waist
and pulled
his legs
and pulled his legs
up
as high
up as high as
they could possibly
go
as they could possibly go
and plunged
my dick
in
and plunged my dick in
up
to the hilt
up to the hilt.

[Untitled]

<pre>
                            I sat
              I sat   on his face
        on his face   I sat on his face
   I sat on his face   I sat on his face,
  I sat on his face,   and he tongued
    and he tongued   my ass
           my ass   and he tongued
    and he tongued   and he tongued my ass
and he tongued my ass   my ass
           my ass   and ate
          and ate   out
             out   my asshole
      my asshole   and ate out
      and ate out   my asshole
      my asshole   and ate out my asshole,
and ate out my asshole,   then I took
      then I took   the tube
        the tube   of KY
          of KY   then I took
      then I took   the tube of KY
    the tube of KY   then I took the tube of KY,
then I took the tube of KY, and smeared it
    and smeared it   on my hand
      on my hand   and smeared it
    and smeared it   on my hand
      on my hand   and smeared it on my hand,
and smeared it on my hand, and eased it
       and eased it   into his asshole
    into his asshole   and eased it
       and eased it   and eased it into his asshole,
and eased it into his asshole, into his asshole
    into his asshole   and I pushed
      and I pushed   and I pushed
      and I pushed   until it was
     until it was   in
             in   up
             up   to the knuckles
   to the knuckles   and I pushed until it was in
and I pushed until it was in up to the knuckles
   up to the knuckles   until it was in up to the knuckles,
until it was in up to the knuckles,

                            then I gently
    then I gently   forced
          forced   then I gently forced
</pre>

then I gently forced
the rest
of the hand
into the opening
then I gently forced
the rest of the hand into the opening
into the opening,
and it slipped
completely
inside
and it slipped
completely inside
and it slipped completely inside,
and the lips
tightened
and the lips tightened
around
my wrist
around my wrist
and the lips tightened around my wrist,
and I slowly
began
to twist
my arm
and I slowly began
to twist my arm
and I slowly began to twist my arm,
and he went
out
of his mind
and he went
out of his mind
and he went out of his mind.

the rest
of the hand
into the opening
then I gently forced
the rest of the hand into the opening
into the opening,
and it slipped
completely
inside
and it slipped
completely inside
and it slipped completely inside,
and the lips
tightened
and the lips tightened
around
my wrist
around my wrist
and the lips tightened around my wrist,
and I slowly
began
to twist
my arm
and I slowly began
to twist my arm
and I slowly began to twist my arm,
and he went
out
of his mind
and he went
out of his mind
and he went out of his mind

BRAINARD-74

Robert Glück

SEX POEM

First I get hot
and then I want to press my crotch to someone else's crotch

each character embraces his characteristic genital

it's so cordial as to be profound

though the man who blows himself's an ourobouros of a different
    color

he says: the more ya drink it the more ya like it if ya can stomach
    it.

I think juices have natural glamour like living next to water

a woman puts a bead of come on her lip in sexual conversation

a peerless language

the sun comes up and a cloud replies with gold

the pianist, pale from classical music,

brings his keyboard mastery to between the sheets

she smiles at him in greek
he hands her a box in Polish

they discover why space is 3 dimensional

They fuck on a round spinning ball

it's simple and it reminds us of life

Though my appeal's not general

a small group of gourmets thinks I'm very sexy

though yes is embarrassing

who'd waste his light saying no beautifully, insincerity the flower
    mouth.

Bob sits on Ed's cock like a hitchhiker singing
I can't give you anything but love

when a drop of sperm hits, his torso shivers like a whip

he says Make my cock your fetish

Then Bob and Ed get kissed by a movie star, abstractly perfect.

In this way my unhappiness challenges their life
framing appetite with a keyhole

The movie star pursues them with a little bow

whose flourish endlessly uncurls into the darkness of farce

Michelangelo's version of Bob's body

Rodin's version of Ed's body

They escape, their sexuality rides them up a boulevard

and turns the signals green to unstrangle the receptive street

MEDITATION: ED

Would you like me to have sex with you
or write a sexy poem about you

putting all my loving lines together

like clouds or sex acts reflected in a teaspoon that measured
a medicine of cherries

With Ed I talk about Ed

his illnesses & his art, his boyhood a bracelet of scissors

in the elementary fragrance of blocks and fingerpaint

and his fertility of dreams.

His body's obviousness and mystery breathe from his
imagination

where friends play themselves and the wind plays an irritating
child

who says: Your lives are haunted because the former tenant was
vain

making love with you in a dream is a solo flight.

Yet I'm brother to love when he wakes up shouting from a
    nightmare

and each jump of the skin over his heart's a victory so tender

that we reach the highest altitude at which simplicity sustains
    life.

Be sincere to Bob and Ed, we are the most beautiful type of all

the simple minded fool.

(Ed just expresses himself better because he deals
with the medium of light.)

Complexity looks at simplicity, a graphic utopia,

a figure with hammer for the heart and anvil for love

and dreaming across it unharmed the little worm that knows
    what to do

If it touches you you should show the surprise and felicity of
    people

whose heart's inwardness discovers the erotic formula

the hot life of the senses:

He's the combination to my safe
he presses to me through the fluid of my eyes:

at the heart of my dream the movement of cinema

a man fights danger for the beautiful woman,

in the fiber of his dream the body of the dreamer

body of cloudy light

POEM
_____

this is my period of sexual meditation

gravity is the way distant objects touch each other

how endlessly shocked they would be at the idea of sex

I am endlessly shocked at the idea of sex like the
falling man who loses the sensation and then depth startles him

the story has a hundred morals but the only
                                    exit is a change of mood

and Bob loves the pleasure he takes in receiving sensation,
when he woke up slowly to a blow job the radio clung to sleep
                                    but its tubes grew redder

he retains it
like the taste of an erotic dream, describe the dream:

a cave where the tides live
two men twist up and up, light gleams off in a rapture
they squeeze liquid from their wet torsos
the deep mystery of the heavenly men

the best looking says, I like men,

any orifice could be a mouth, in bed everything that's
not me is you, I like earth men,

they are always surprised at sex, interest lights up their eyes,
the most jaded, innocent as a prisoner, turns his head in wonder.

A situation stares Bob in the eyes as he approaches and
continues staring into his eyes through the back of his head.
If my mind's touched I'm totally touched

Bob says We might as well go all the way

Ed says I love conclusions, when I come I get
a heart attack a stroke and four flat tires

Bob says By any chance do you know basic syncopation?

Ed says A man was embraced and embraced

Bob says New hope to my hands

Ed's forehead wrinkles to understand
he says, the empty whiteness moves down the stairs,
the blind panther, a room appears as he enters it

Then Bob shared the surprise of
people who become what they don't expect

then we take a shower where I love to drink water off his skin

Paul Goodman

FOR G., AET. 16

"You're beautiful," I said, "I love you."
I met him half an hour ago
but he was and I did—
there were above a hundred thousand people
at the party and he was a bar-tender.
"Am I?" he said, "I don't know what to say—"
Since he didn't know me at all
he could hardly know that I was serious,
that I hoped he would be happy
as he no doubt deserved
because of his blue eyes and flowing hair;
and I wished that I could be one
who would make him happy.

I entertained even the wan idea
that I too in being one
to make him happy might be happy.
Instead I gave him my little lecture
on how to live cheaply in Hawaii
which isn't where I am going
and I kissed him despairingly
on the mouth and he said good-bye.
"Maybe," he said, "we'll see each other
another time." What did he mean by that?

"No, Ronny, sit and talk.
Let's skip the sex. I'll buy your beer.
What good are your muscular arms
if you won't hold onto me?
I see your cock is hard
but you'll lie there like a lamp post."

Yet he was not ridiculous.
He kept his glum green eyes averted.
They looked at me dartingly.
His forehead was perplexed.
His solid frame was mute
but had a mute appeal that was alive.
He didn't want to go away. I said:
"Try to say it. What are you thinking of?
I'll find you words." I guessed that he would bawl
if father treated him gentle for a change.

He said, "I'm not thinkin about anythin.
Ast me a question so I have somethin to say.
Mostly when I sit like this I am
not thinkin about anythin at all.
Maybe I'm thinkin about so many things
I dunno what I'm thinkin about, it's sub
conscious, maybe."

                           "Don't you ever cry?"
His eyes were scalding hot; connecting sentences
opened the abyss of making sense
which he could ill afford. "Naw, I don't cry."
"What's bad about crying?" "Nothin's bad,
only you ast me, no, I never cry."
"Don't you feel like crying now, Ronny?"
"Naw, I don't feel it," Ronny said and wept
—one tear and panicked. "Why do you bother?
why is everybody innerested in *me?*
I'm just one o the fellers."

                                    The conceit
shone brilliantly out of his sidelong leer,
he waited baited for a compliment,
his long hair was combed Puerto Rican style.

"Suppose you could, what would you like to do?"
"You'll laugh at me," he said. "No, I won't laugh."
"I'd like to be an actor." "Marlon Brando?"
"I don' need to imitate Marlon Brando,"
he said indignantly, "I'll act myself!"
"Why don't you?" "I am waitin to be discovered."

[*Untitled*]

For great pebbles the beach at Middle Cove
Newfoundland! They fitted the palm
like baseballs, you hurled them into the sea.
Many maroon, most were gray,
green when I wet them with my tongue
crawling on hands and knees to lick the stones,
and God were they smooth. I am desperately
in love with this tangible, as I grow old,
belly balls and buttocks world, David.

[*Untitled*]

Like an angel: the piano light
   glinting in his aureole hair
sticking out the tip of his tongue
   he picks on his guitar

—one is no longer supposed to see
   these pre-Raphael images
but watching him through the window
   so it is, so it is.

Be precise. The wonder lasts
   only an hour in the woe
and storm of nineteen-seventy
   but it is so, it has been so.

I am pleased with myself tonight
   a veteran I am not shot
when he fucked me it felt sweet
   and my own hard-on was hot.

Therefore in Victorian stanzas
   riming the second with the fourth
I will praise the nature of things
   in my pretty home in the north.

That lute song of the sixteenth century
   though Spanish was international
like the famous fight between the fleets
   —men make war too in international style.

A PLANE TO PITTSBURGH

The ills of this world are mathematical, as Kafka said. I notice
3 fellows boarding the plane that I'd like to sit next to me, but
the 96 seats are assigned at random, and even discounting the
pairs who sit together, the odds against my happiness are over-
whelming. So it proves.

Oh, I keep at it. Disturbing my obnoxious seat-mate, I get up and
walk the aisle and ask for a match. I beat my brain for a pretext
to exchange seats, but nothing is plausible. Anyway the weather
is rough and the pilot keeps flashing "Fasten seat belts."

So I give up and write these sentences to pass the time, to make
do. The evils of this world are mathematical, they are mathematical. The goods, I have found, don't fall into my lap. Some
people have a lot of luck. Others, worse off than I, don't have
a chance even to make an effort.

The blond with the squinty eyes was best, though not the best-
looking. Blue collar class. There's quicker savvy in a boy
like that. For a short flight. And there's Pittsburgh. Yes, and
another thing: the lower class boy would have had less prejudice
against how old I am. He would have fewer notions.

Kafka himself was in the actuarial business. He *would* know.

Steve Jonas

AN ODE FOR GARCIA LORCA

In New Orleans Walt Whitman was married.
An Anglican priest duly performed the dark rite.
sub rosa. The Mint paid. So did the Butterflies
    and Lesbian sparrows. (coined from old metal)
The Ceremony took place—slowly—in the shade!
Creole ladies avoided the sun like the plague.
'cadjuns', being the only pure stock,
                farmed their boys out like studs.
These are Walt Whitman's children. And here,
    to convince you, is a photograph. A dirty
photograph. Beneath huey long's bridge,
      the which consumed ten hershey bars; The Pair
stripped to the waist, standing in drains:
The Sun upon their belly buttons. Outsized,
(these pictures always exaggerate) low hanging cloud for
    adjective.
The bride's maid, with a bunch of pansies, (fades) were
      graciously received. There are no differences here!
There are also his children and, in case I didnt warn you,
this is a poem.
The background is a blurr about the horizon.
Note: In a photograph the foreground is by that time
      background, (adding "not really" to it).
        It's Five O'clock.
        It gets dark early.
        I cant see to finish this.

DISCOURSE

In Plato's dialogues
                    Socrates spoke
        of that love enraging youth
    to exceed the speed limits
                    set by law
    or when lacking motor vehicles they
            rape, (which is a joke) or plunder
    drug stores
                    cigarette or other
                            vending machines
    for nickles & dimes which,
            if not in the meantime apprehended by
        the all efficient
                            local police, they
        lavish on teenage girls with snatches
    chockd full ov giggles. Properly channeld
    of course this energy could be
                            directed
            into color design if not
        to the arrangement of particulars
    in the pending,
                    eagerly anticipated,
                American Poem. But then
    he was an old man
                        when he spoke thus
        so why smite the breast
                    thinking to rebuke the soul. Besides
        his boys were
                mostly fops imbued
    with their high toned *aretē* which
    could never apply in this
            our so late Republic where
                        dogs and cats stand,
    tails between their legs to await
            the low of equal dispensation. It's as tho
        within the organic structure,
    gangrene has long set in.
                            1961

BLACKSTONE PARK

Dans le vieux parc solitaire et glacé

in this park of dilapidated times
　　where no one comes save
　　　　　the bums & those
who love beneath the vine or the rose

winos toss empty pints
　　　on-to the half shell of
a no longer running fount
dry voices of castrated hopes

complain to a jagged moon
　　　　in its final resolve
at the last bench of a row
　　　two shadows equivocate

they have no sex nor time
their words are witherd grasses
　　　beneath the shuddering night;
some old ecstasy performed for fools

who believe the words they've said
　　　　when the wind is down
and the green innocence of death
　　　stalks the place

with a rattle of two elevated cars
　　　overhead　　hang-dog
and headed for the suburbs

1966

as snow flying past
            on the picture tube
& petals of ten thousand springs
            carried by the wind
blowing no good
                  then the fade-out
                  & I turn to drink.
Pair of kingfishers shack up in
      the pavilion with rotten teeth
stoned bi-sexual unicorns
            case the park &
the thud-like empty tomb
            (to each his own
                  after his kind or a folded
                              quilt)
to think I let an underpaid
            pencil pushing bureaucratic
                        appointment deter me
from a here she goes fire one
            (just ripe for making)

                  plum blossoms

                  Tu Fu (713–770)

[*The Esplanade is a well-known gay cruising area in Boston. —Ed.*]

POEM

It's a dull poem
    whose finish
           is sex

& whose climax
         is spoonful
of angelic
        gissom
    flush'd down
the drain
        in a men's room
where hopeful in-
        vitations come
at you from slabs of marble in-
viting
      Travel
        69
   or trips around the world!
just call this below number
         & we must assume
              centrally lo-
cated under 21
          white males
& i'll be yr slave

1965

E. A. Lacey

TWO POEMS FOR LEOBARDO

1. Your body here beside me, warm and still
   this morning, as so many mornings now;
   still webbed in sleep the dusty face; the smooth
   boy's arms are crossed upon the hairless chest;
   only the heart beats the stomach's tender drum;
   the genitals at peace; the strong legs curl
   hunched against mine.
   Surrendered to the other violence of sleep,
   you make no protest as my roaming fingers
   explore you, alien continent. I know
   your body in the act, not in repose; I do not
   know you at all.
   The furrow of a dream now cuts your forehead,
   for you are travelling in distant places;
   the future for you has the shape of dreams,
   for me, the shape of time.

2. Far away now I sleep, my little one.
   I do not have the smooth silk of your skin
   to wrap me in
   but huddle curled up in a dense cocoon
   of memories and wishes and regrets.
   I am getting older fast; my hair is falling;
   though in myself I feel I cannot age;
   I drink too much, and there are clinical signs
   of some sort of malaise in the whole organism.
   Also the tropical climate does not agree with me.
   Do I bore you with details? There are many palm trees here.
   The dark people are kind. The nights are warm.
   But you were warmer.

Hawks and eagles!
Red and black ones!
Gold and white ones!
Yellow and green ones!
Captive, for sale on the beach at Copacabana!
Three feet from wing-tip to cloth wing-tip they measure,
poised sharp bodies, cruel hieratic faces,
outspread wings of cloth ready for flight.
Three thousand cruzeiros a kite, and the man who makes them
sits cross-legged, fat, unaquiline, feet rooted in sand,
on the beach in front of the tourist hotel,
old-womanishly sewing and stitching, answering the tourists'
    questions.
Around him the blue-and-gold afternoon, cliff-shadows of
    buildings advancing now across the white sands of
    Copacabana,
and a scurry of brown young half-naked helpers who, when they
    aren't assisting him,
jump in and out of the surf, scuffle at soccer, ogle the girls,
or run along the beach to the other hotels
hawking their wares.

These fly too, these eagles, mocking their cloth,
fly briefly, touched with sun, arched over beach and bathers,
fly high in the afternoon wind that comes in from the open sea,
in a wind that too soon dies away, draws them to earth again;
but if you're young and agile and a kite-maker's helper
you can keep them up in the air in their blaze of colour for almost
    an afternoon,
running along the beach, snaring the wind.

You fly too,
young hawk boys of Copacabana,
your brown rapacious bodies circling sunlit over mine,
hungry, hunting for sex, for money, for experience,
in afternoons of sun and sea and wind that are all one afternoon;
but the long shadow crawls indelible across the sand,

and there is a secret no one will ever tell you, but you will
    learn it, kite-boys,
seeking the sun and not reaching it,
wanting the world and not getting it,
nor knowing why your flight must be as brief as your cloth birds'
    flying:
one eagle moment bright in the sun, and then the slow going-
    down to the end of all flight,
to sticks and rags and tattered colours fading,
and darkness and old age.

GUATEMALA

When I see boys leap barefoot from a train,
their bold cheeks glowing in cold mountain air,
and know that I shall not come here again
to see them, hear them, touch them, feel their tangled hair;
when I watch their carved alien features, study
what the world is to them, and how defined
—why do I want to possess every body,
to live each life, to think with each one's mind?

Now they recede into their distant towns,
into old age, and deaths in obscure places;
boys that I might have slept with, drunk with, lived beside
dissolving into unremembered faces;
and time and the train's rhythm steady ride
and draw me back into myself, and down.

Young Inca boy with a guitar:
the dark waterfall of your hair
splashed over me as we made love;
your body, slim and arched, above
me darted in and out
of my well-trained and willing mouth
until the salt sweet sperm came; then
at peace, accomplices and men,
we licked each other's sweaty skin,
confessed our prides and told our sins,
—a poet growing old, a young
confusion with a life-style — song —
and then sleep came and brought us dreams
of childhood, in each other's arms.

The gold of bodies does not melt;
preserves itself in what was felt.

Moroccan boys in mountain towns:
djellabas, snow-white or leaf-brown,
hid slim white cocks that like sharp knives
cut my ass; then the cool kif pipes;
Mexican boys, met on the road,
in jails, cantinas, briefly had
and disremembered; dusty faces,
small cocks, tight balls, great eagernesses;
Argentines, Uruguayans, complex
city boys needing simple sex;
treacherous, delicate Indian lads
from beautiful, deadly Trinidad;
—all of you are dimly with me yet;
I keep the faith; I do not forget.

The gold of bodies does not melt;
preserves itself in what was felt.

Brazilian boys with laughing cocks
earnest with need to get your rocks
off in some way, and set your seal
on woman, man or animal;
Dário, Fabrício, Adonai
—you will not age, you will not die;
my mind will keep you always young,
brown-skinned and eager and well-hung;
kisses you did not have to give,
and gave, I, while I live,
will recall, and how you would lie
beside me afterwards, till the sky
went white, and the bem-te-vi at dawn
woke us with his three-note song.

The gold of bodies does not melt;
preserves itself in what was felt.

This is not boasting, for who cares
these days? I have made love in cars,
especially taxis (always prefer
cabbies and shine-boys; they're quick and sure),
on beds and hillsides, in ruined churches,
on beaches, mountain-tops, under bridges;
and though I happen to dote on boys,
like Jews who've nothing against goys
I hold no brief against the man
who lies with girl, sow, ewe, or ram;
and, growing older, only enthuse
for money, to keep on buying youths
to warm my age with their hot hands:
the best loves are one-night stands!

The gold of bodies does not melt;
preserves itself in what was felt.

Seven years ago, almost to the month and day.

It is not hard to pick a sailor up at Retiro Station.
They come in, hot and penniless, from the sex prison of their
    ships and the time prison of the sea,
ready to sleep anywhere, or do anything,
to the great city, grave city on the silver river
—the city that hides its loneliness in eating.
Even out of uniform, you can pick them out by their air of guilt
    and expectancy,
as they arrive in pairs at the plaza, eye the prospects, then
    separate,
loll on the grass, sprawl on benches, prowl the marble station,
circle the British clock tower, round and round, like a ship's
    deck,
with faintly rolling gait.
Conversation is easy. Sit down beside one on the park bench.
Ask him where he comes from, tell him you once passed through
    there on a train, offer him a cigarette, offer . . .
Brown country boys, desert sailors most of them, drafted and
    recruited
from Tucuman, Jujuy, Saltá, towns of the mestizo north,
they come to the park because they are sick of the sea and afraid
    of the city and Retiro at least reminds them of home,
as it vomits out all day the hopeful brown faces arriving from the
    country
to the dark city, sad city, cold city on the silver river.
Once you have picked one up, the search for a room:
the good hotels have fastidious doormen who look at you
    unnervingly;
the alojamientos have stereos and mirrors for men with women;
the hospedajes demand many documents and show you sex-
    perfumed cots in rooms for five.
Finally, success. Inside the room. Alone.
The touching of bodies. The bedding down. Lifebuoyed
clean smell of white-and-blue crinkly uniform, soon cast aside,
    then of firm young body

trembling cock already rampant, casting its shadow on the hard
    brown belly,
and a desire for human tenderness.

O all night in that boy's arms I lay after the tumbling,
as he slept with an erection, and in the morning did him again,
for the price of a pack of cigarettes and a hotel room.
Eighteen years old, from Mendoza, in the throes of sex and life.
He had been a naval cadet for just five months.
Soon he would sail away—in a week—for the Antarctic; he was
    afraid; he had never been there; was it really cold?
And did I want to meet him again Sunday night?
And as we rode back in the subway, returning to Retiro,
morning light hurting our eyes, ill-humoured city faces
    all around us, we filled with sleep and peacefulness,
the question, almost whispered: "Te gusté?" "Did you like me?"

Sunday night I got stupidly drunk, did not go to Retiro;
alcohol ruins the best moments of a manic-depressive, or
    perhaps instinctively
I didn't want to spoil it. Never saw him again.
Seven years ago that sailor set forth for Antarctica.

[*Retiro is the largest of the train stations in Buenos Aires. —Ed.*]

VERACRUZ (*#2 from "Mexico South"*)

for Paulinho

After so many years absent, visiting you again, old whore of a
    city,
old cunt that opened for Cortés and his invading horses and
    hordes, and began the gestation of a new world sired by
    priests, nobles and jailbirds on heart-eaters, pyramid-
    builders and peasants,
I recognise you, city, from somewhere else. The same heat, the
    same sea,
the noises, winds and stinks, the sensual torpor, the avenues of
    phallic palms,
the same shoe-shine boys who three times a week polished my
    shoes

- or is it their younger brothers, or am I just getting older?
The same sidewalk cafes, though here slightly more musical,
     awash with sounds of mariachis and marimbas,
and crowded along the plazas instead of along the beaches,
but thronged by the same mildly bewildered American and
     Western-European tourists,
trying to enjoy themselves and not quite succeeding,
sympathetic yet faintly ridiculous, like pale Northern fish cast up
     flopping on some tropical strand,
wondering, probably, how they have got so far from home and
     into such an alien environment, and what to do about the
     situation.
The bars give out free lunches in abundance to everyone, only
     complicating the tourists' embarrassment
when the shrimp soup turns out too peppery to drink, and the
     pieces of shell left (deliberately?) in the stuffed crab break
     fragile molars.
Tristesse de voyage. And at night, in the starless heat, along the
     malecón,
the boys looking for girls and girls waiting for boys
stroll, meet, converse, play guitars in groups for hours, unmolested;
and the men looking for boys and boys waiting for men
sit slightly further away, on the more distant benches,
or lean against lampposts, gently, languidly playing with
     themselves.
And suddenly it is you, Rio de Janeiro; I am in Cinelândia
casing the hustlers — which will rob me, which will not? — which
     is well-hung, which is not?
or walking the night streets of Copacabana, along the sea-front,
     under the burnt-out street-lights,
looking for Paulinho or Dario or Betinho or any other 15- or
     16-year-old chicken to share my sheets and flesh with:
pick out, pick up, pick on, pick over, pick apart — throw away.
La chair est triste, hélas, et j'ai lu tous les livres,
and all desire is sorrow and all places are the same place,
and bodies mate but do not meet and all this has been said
a thousand times before and better, and I can add only one thing
- that the distance from here to there and from now to then
is that from me to you and is unbridgeable
- even by the True Cross.

Michael Lally

THEIR IMAGINATION SAFE

you, wing like across the bright animals

       I taste the metal of my death, your tongue

(remember Sonny Rollins blowing with Thelonious Monk
                            at the Five Spot

        one foot stiffens with muscle cramp

                on your tongue
                that dark inside
                we love to fill
                but pray each day
                will open up to someone new
                & beautiful & loose like dreams

      my mouth opens up like a floor, walk around in it

flash cards:
OPEN / RELAX / LIE BACK / WIDER / RELAX / BE FILLED
          we are fine together, one safe smell
              in it the metal of what dies in us each day
              the rinse of knowing who we are
                  what honor we can give
                    they are afraid to know

     brother, stretch across my map your face & ass & toes
       insert your A's & B's into my Y's & Z's
         lie back again with me before we go
           & go with me to where they cant imagine
           taste death & know what they cannot know
           we are each other's children   alchemists
                                  midwives
                                  peasants

in each other's crevices creating seed from shit & loving it

(there are those who have never been afraid of the dark   )

I am wide & divided as vulnerable as a lamb to be stroked or
    slaughtered
& you slaughter me with the stroke of your tongue & cheek at
    my cheek &
cheek & reach of dark between

                              where is the machine invented to
                                  capture this art

                                  in our hearts brothers
                                      in our hearts

NOW

Wanting to be Humphrey Bogart for 30 years
finding out youre more like Lauren Bacall.

but

imitation, assimilation, alchemy
hermaphrodites were strong symbols of
alchemist "magic" not symbols: were

                          wings held close to the bone
                          left foot on the block
                          right foot in the atmosphere
                          hand held

I come out with myself & find

                          everyone

Gerrit Lansing

AMAGING GRACE AND A SALAD BOWL:

in memory of Stephen Jonas

> . . . And of the dead,
> the dear gone new into the ancient halls,
> > "the melody lingers on"
> —a favorite quote of his—
> > his melodies do.

> > Is no repair on earth
> > for broken nerves,
> > wornout heads, the injuries the sensitives
> > > self-inflict.
> The god of this world treads on brains like grapes.
> In the winepress what can we do but sing
> > if we are men at all.

1.

> > you are gone Esteban
> & yr big brown body just isn't there to hands you chose,
> > Hotel Madison men's room boys,
> weird high objects of yr unearthly love,
> dumb credit card thieves, boosters, drunks,
> the last junk of the world.
> > They shift without you on the esplanade,
> > and I shift without you, like yr other friends,
> who have their own memories of yr kindness, cooking, talk,
> > yr body that changed and changed.

2.

> > I have a salad bowl,
> > unpolished wood
> > > I cherish as of you best memory.
> > The courtesy and purity of greens,
> > lemon juice and olive oil.

You wove a fabric beyond yr words,
ideas I sometimes felt were crazy,
a coat of hospitality,
embracing wine and merriment,
of Boston dawn, the place of time you loved.

3.

Boston you were to me, after I left New York
hub of, haven.
Would pile in exhausted from nights of pleasure,
to hear yr morning chatter,
drink coffee, sometimes beer or wine.
You knew the Boston crevices, their histories, the rats,
and marketplace,
how to get electric free,
clothes, hi fi parts, good affabilities.

4.

'Du musst dein Leben ändern' Rilke wrote,
& how poesy transforms we disputed oft,
not denying that it does, it sure does.

Now, sunset fading, I wonder what the panoply of spring
was worth to all of us,
the price of all that agony, the sky on fire.
Boys moving through the blood, the witless loves,
the loved ejaculations and again again the upturned wild
faces.

For you, a reason found in madness, a cap on mere
existence.

You denied the ecstasy I claimed,
said tricks were only tricks,
which I in turn denied,
but you and I together knew

bright words hanging on the boughs of dawn.

Amazing grace.

ALBA

"That was the clock.
I have to go."

"Twenty minutes more in bed.
My body's warm, the air is cool."

"I've got to be at work by nine."

"I kiss your legendary throat.
When love's at work the world is sunk beneath the sea.

Press your body onto me.
See,
We flow together like molten gold and molten gold."

A GHAZEL OF ABSENCE

for D.

If I had trained a gull
I'd send it off to Booth Bay Harbor
(like Solomon to Sheba, like Hafiz to his Friend)
bearing greetings & compleynts of absence
from "the cypress envying your figure & the moon bowled
                              over by your face."
The bird would say: *you there, captain,*
though you are absconditus my heart is touching you

sunrise to sunset the winds weave endlessly between us
& let of my Affection the boiling deepsea currents testify.

Lest the warriors of grief ravage your beauty (la Beauté)
I send you the ransom of my self-love, keep it,

musicians will play out Gerrit's desire
in the mode of this poem which is like a "gazelle."

Furtively, then freely,
they made it in an empty boxcar,
moonlight streaming in the open door,
two o'clock in the morning,
relaxing,
each eager for the other's pleasure,
faster and faster,
mouths to bodies fastened,
enjoyment like forever and then at the same time time shot
off into eternity's gullet.

Stars strung out like mistletoe over a heavy sky,
peace, the necessary return to normal economy, being
what each one was and is, kisses of satisfied friendship.

3 from COCK HAIKU

The Forest Ranger in Springtime

naked in the sun
alone on Lone Cloud Mountain
his warm cock erect

Bright Day, Parents Away

behind white garage
the boys unzip their levis
quick grab eager cocks

Dingy Hotel Room Scene

shade drawn clothes off, points
to himself, grin for new friend:
"this cock crows at night."

Winston Leyland

GAY POETS

Angels of the Dawn
Angels of Light
Angels of Delight
Angels of Lightning
Angels of the Lyre
   Apollos Ascending
   Orpheuses Descending
Androgynous Angels
Bastard Angels
Angels in Drag
Angels of Desolation
Angels of Liberation

Gay Poets

                        5/75

AMATITLAN

for Miguel

Your Mayan kisses
   ocean spray
Your lithe body pressed
   against.

Silent
    parting.

   now in me, you,
   like a spring

                    1/75

ANGEL METAMORPHOSIS

Hundred water flesh knowing the Omega
Angel busted, your pain re-adhered
Angel pronounce alleys: with drops
    most mornings name the eyes
Seashore angel scare that began with
    sure shocked friends floating easily
And I walk clutter fire the eyelids
    because you are open skin
Some nine I look down pain eyes

Dec. 1969

MEMORY RECAPTURED

after a poem by Stephen Spender

Even while I write him I am remembering
the quick laugh of the clear blue eyes,
the quiet but intense gaze of concern.
Even while I write I remember, for love dips
what it experiences into a flood of memory
vaster than itself. Thus what I recall I
shall so always: the glint of the quick lids,
the golden hair and the warm, surprised smile.
These shall remain imprinted indelibly on my mind.
They shall remain when my life lies with no past
or future but only endless space. When I behold
hope and despair, the sweet words the enigmatic
smile will remain. These were his marks indelible:
an empathic mind and that clear glance,
which made all else forgiven.

June 1968

"Hermaphrodite-Angel of Peladan": *drawing by Czanara*

Gerard Malanga

NUMBERS

for john rechy

i am with numbers at the frozen arena with the nameless
    encounter
it is 12 oclock noon the bodies single file walking in silence
the bodies sitting on fenders of parked cars   the bodies of fire
    and silence
i am with numbers at the magic place burned in disaster
that each of us wears
i am with numbers at a quarter past three
at the summit at the ritual dance
at the numbers of bodies sending out signals
the unbuttoned jeans at the waist
the bare shoulder that points to the spot in agreement
the language of eyes the circle of the unbroken
i am with numbers who gives me his hand when i fall
the blazing moment
i am with numbers with the numbers in dance
with the numbers of minutes elapsed and evolving
i am with numbers at 5.30 p.m. as our bodies descend with the
    sun
with bodies moving into the shadows with shadows moving
    into the numbers
i am with numbers walking from one piece of ground to the next
    in a place between darkness and light

                                   18:ii:73   los angeles

COMING OF AGE

for tony pinck on the occasion
of his 18th birthday

sometimes its inconceivable that you should be the age you are
though i have long wondered what it would be like to be you now
except for the things i would do differently the way you could
not decide for yourself that things were not in the flow
i write as though you could understand
what have you learned what can you remember
one must always pretend something among the young in silence
but in which of my years will you see yourself tomorrow
perhaps nothing for some time will attach itself to your life
i leave you my fate as a storm warning without what it takes to
    live
inside the poem that must grow out of a pain it never brought
but i say to myself you are not a child now
whatever you have to do has not yet begun
now i forget where the difference falls
and the end i suppose is not yet

20:x:71   nyc

Paul Mariah

QUARRY / ROCK:
A REALITY POEM
IN THE TRADITION OF GENET

I.
O, Seeger, the night you tied the cabbie
to the tree
           and shot him, did you know
the shadow of the chair was waiting for you?
You, murderer, guillotined one,
You of the severed head,
You on death row for seven years,
You six feet seven taker of life
you with the death shrouded head.

One night you walking in line
to your cell, swung and touched
hands with your love, Stevie.
You two walking in line
to your cells, swung and touched
hands. Swung hands and touched
the only way you could say good-night
swung hands and touched.

Later, that same night Stevie
lying in his 6 by 9 cell
in the quiet one-man cell
in the quiet of his only home
his desires became rampant
wanting you wanting
wanting you touching him wanting

(O, Seeger, what have they done to Stevie?
What have they done to Stevie?)

(The County had said his voyeur eyes
were too blue and should be
put away until the color changed to grey)

wanting you wanting
wanting you touching him wanting

the broom became you
the broom became the strength of you
the broom became the anal worship of you
the broom became the regular stroke of you
the broom became the reality of you

until he fell off the bed
and broke
            the broom off, inside where
you were in the quiet of his night
he was visited by red horror
not withstanding, not waking

II.
O, Seeger, the night you tied the cabbie
to the tree
            and shot him, did you know . . .

that you would wait seven years
to be strapped in a chair?

that they would kill your love
in isolation, in lonely isolation?

that in the cubicle of a cell you
would want him, would want to love him?

It was the evening after you knew
Stevie had died that I heard

green tears whimper from your cell
and knew that in that severed head

you still had human tears.

(O, Seeger, what have they done to Stevie?
What have they done to Stevie?)

Later, when Stevie was taken
to pauper's field where dandelions
grow in reverence to the sun.

When his parents refused his body,
refused their son. It was then
I heard you rage like a wild tiger.

In the cold antigone of your dreams
I saw you in defiance go out
and bury the body. And in revenge
you took to the fields
looking for his parents
hiding in the forest of your dreams
in cabbie clothing.

O, Seeger, the night you tied the cabbie
to the tree
            and shot him, did you know
you still had green tears?

Lino cut by Samuel Reese

IMAGINARY LETTER OF YOUNG CAESAR
ON THE BITHYNIAN TOUR 81 B.C.

The Sun is in Virgo.

My Dear Nicomedes,

Yesterday was your birthday
I regret that I could not be there
in attendance at your celebration.
I had to work
for the State. They do not recognize
unfamiliar days, unless it is that
of a Saint too long forgotten
(the philosopher, Saint Hildegard
of Bingen, never canonized . . .)

Exiled from Rome, my strategy
is to capture Lesbos. Then,
Rome will welcome me back
into her arms. It is your arms
I would rather be welcome in
But we cannot confine our love
to those states. You taught me that.
Master teacher that you are.
We will be sailing
as soon as the food for the journey
is gathered, brought to the ships
and stored. Perhaps,
when all is quiet tonight
I will sneak in to be with you,
to lie with you for a few hours.
But I must be back at the ships
before the sun arises. I will bear
the gift of an eagle spread
whole when I come tonight.

> With love,
> Julio

THE SPOON RING

He had the silver
Handle of a spoon
Curled around
His finger.

His grandmother's
Silver,
A wedding present,
To preserve

The family crest.
The spoon ring
That I wear wings
Me back to prison.

The secret vows
Of prisoners
Exchange rings,
Silver contraband.

(Whenever a spoon
Is stolen from chow
Line, frisks happen,
Search for lost silver

Either a shiv appears
In some hidden corner
Or a lover announces
His Bond, shows his hand.)

He did not know
The ritual of silver
As he showed me
His grandmother's ware.

A spoon, a wedding ring,
Crest of prison despair
That knows the ritual song
'To Spoon the Empty Air.'

TEXTURES

1. Brushwork

Thru yr soft hands
I become pliable
And you sculpt
Me into yr being.

2. Heat

Thru tension
I feel assault on my body
And know that you are making me
Yrs. Forever and ever,
And then one day more:
Even if it is only for tomorrow
Or this: One Hour

3. Pulse

Yr hands
Say
The things
You forget
To say
The things
Yr hands
Say.

4. Sight

The eyes shine in defiance
Of the glaring sun.
            Only the moon
knows the negligence
Of saying things.

5. Act

My body which you make

Moist with yr lips
Swerves in eddies of delight
And falls back again to wet sheets,
Drained dry of starlustre
You swallowed,
            for me,
Loved.

THE FIGA

I want you to know
how it feels
to have a fist
the size of a poem
up yr ass.
Get the vaseline.
This is one finger
and if I angle right
I can get past the knuckle
Hold still
This is two fingers
Introduce rhythm
fingermovements
allow the play to contine
This is three fingers
keep the rhythm steady
never stop the movement
I want you to feel the size
this is four fingers
cupped & the play continues
and I am not going to stop
Lift the left leg higher
This is my thumb
and the movement is steady
my fingers move into

you are closing in
around my wrist.
How does it feel
to have a poem
shoved up your ass
the size of a fist?
Now I am going to open
my palm and make
a scratch on the inside.
This was the scene
and I had to get
out of bed to write it
so you would know
the size of it
and now we can go on
gently, lovingly.

Wayne McNeill

I WONDER IF VERLAINE HELD RIMBAUD

I wonder if Verlaine held Rimbaud
like this, slowly rocking the troubled
head, wild with curls.

                (Rimbaud murmured,
Verlaine merely smiled
as a wind rose to set them
walking from the park,
far from the stars that drove
poor Arthur into another's arms.)

In our room
a mushroom candle
flickers in the corner,
keeping Night
at a safe distance.

             (Outside,
the humans keep to themselves,
sometimes pressing their
noses to the glass.)

Taylor Mead

AUTOBIOGRAPHY [*after a poem by Ferlinghetti*]

I have blown
And been blown
I have never had a woman
I have been in great jails and terrible jails
the great jails were the tanks
and the terrible jails were the model prisons.
I have seen my mother a few hours before she died.
I have seen my father pinching pennies and felt it.
I have heard and felt my father in his worship of
    money worshipping money and the U.S.A. of money
    madness, fuck it!
I have been beaten nearly to death before an
    "enlightened" Greenwich Village crowd.
I have been beaten in my hospital bed by sadistic
    doctors.
I have been arrested by a jealous policewoman and
    I should have hit her and killed her.
I have played all the pianos that all the famous
    pianists have played in Carnegie Hall in the basement
    of Steinway Hall and I still play them
    after making it with the elevator boys on a quiet
    religious Sunday afternoon.
I have made goo goo eyes at Marlon Brando with no
    luck
    but not too much discouragement either.
I have made it with Montgomery Clift in Central Park
    against a little pagoda
    or at least he said it was Montgomery Clift and
    it was Montgomery Clift too.
Elizabeth Taylor has really looked at me from under
    a veil on Fifth Avenue and Susan Strasberg and
    Judith Anderson all on Fifth Avenue and can't

remember her name on Sixth Avenue now the
Avenue of the Americas and then too
And that year's winner of the Antoinette Perry
award followed me from the St. Regis where he lived
and I've never been in for four blocks until
I regretfully lost him because I'm shy.
And my first day alone in New York almost this famous
cowboy star made goo goo eyes at me on the steps
of the New York Public Library, main branch
And I went into the Times Square Duffy Square
subterranean toilet with one of the movies' Tarzans
and he showed his big peter
and I showed him my small one
because it was cold and
I didn't want to get it excited unless I was sure
something great was about to take place
And it didn't.

[*Untitled*]

Incredible
Crotch-burning child light
tan almost white bulging
long pants there in center
bulge almost bursting
my eyelids throat
lick you across subway
aisle filling subway
car with your gyzm
everyone swimming
drowning swallowing
doors open at next
station everyone recovers
and goes home

[Untitled]

I wrote this poem
in Venice to the lion
with the wings
by the Doge's
Palace which has
2 windows different
and makes the whole
thing and the husky
gondoliers rape me
in their boats with
black pants and
shoulders and oars
and under bridges
at all times of
the day while the
tourists don't know
what to say or do
and laugh a
little and go home
happy—huge
masculine boats
dock at my door
waiting to fuck
me with diesel
engines and flags

and windows while
I squirm and hurt
and can't really
take it sometimes—
all too rough and
tumble and giving me
cancer of the ass but
I don't care—die die
die is the word—
I even forgive
Orion and Joe
and Estelle for
hating me
really—they are
good people—
at least different
and handsome in
a freak way.
Venice is full
of water and murky
people who are
all afraid of themselves
and are hopeless.

Give me your poor, your tired—and let me blow them.

*   *   *

I dreamt last night I was blowing Jack Kerouac but he
had so much he couldn't come—in fact no one could
make him come anymore.

*   *   *

I was Queen for a Dago.

*   *   *

In Lynchburg, Virginia a man took me home and blowed me
for the first time when I was 19. When he didn't die
I said "hmm."

*   *   *

The God Jupiter himself was homosexual, and his lover
was his handsome cup bearer—Ganymede, that an eagle
brought to heaven for him.

*   *   *

Bette Davis in *Beyond the Forest.*—She is too good.

*   *   *

radio commercial:
"What's the best thirst quencher to keep on hand that
everybody can enjoy?"
Answer: a man

*   *   *

Give us this day our daily bed-companion.

*   *   *

I'm sick of fairies pretending not to be fairies—no
fairy should be ashamed of its wings.

*   *   *

There's nothing so fey as a reformed gay.

*   *   *

Lately I've been getting a desire to push these big beautiful
studs off cliffs rather than go to bed with them.

*   .   *   *

"Wanda Landowska is dead and I'll never be able to
suck assholes to harpsichord music again." M.G.

*   *   *

*   *   *

On a little Amphetamine in a glass of water I can write
Naked Breakfast, Lunch and Dinner.

*   *   *

This British sailor says I have Gertrude Stein eyes.

[*Untitled*]

Young grooving
fart-maddened hero
attacks 12 year old
slave-boy Taylor Mead
in Port Said tent
city shoe shine parlor
—broken bottles
everywhere from
the terrible resistance
the hopeless slave-boy
put up against
his 6 foot 2 190 pound
attacker
the police were
unable to separate
the combatants and
they were sold as
a single piece on
the auction block
the following Tuesday
at the end of the line
out at fair fields
on the ocean
Andre Gide was
the purchaser
and Picasso's
painting—the girl
in the mirror was
inspired directly
by their pieces.

Thomas Meyer

BOY MUSE,
URANIAN ROSES FOR STRATO
[selections]

Naked thigh—
lightning eye.

A boy's well-knit
body—

Love's net

    *   *

Your looks
keep old men
awake all night.

The spells
you weave
bring the sea
to the shore.

    *   *

Was it
a swarm of bees,
a patch of nettles
a roaring fire or

just his glance?

    *   *

Hard as I try
to look the other way
I hardly get by
before my eyes
are over my shoulder.

    *   *

He's back!

with hair on his legs . . .

* *

David at my arms
Michael singing to me,
Edward on my knee,
Kenneth boiling my cod,
Allen simmering my beans,
Phillip with carrots in his lap,
John whispering in my ears,
Mark tickling my nipples—

Boys,
that's an antipasto!

* . *

Sunburnt boy   Tender sapling
be my sun   bend for me.

* *   * *

Gentle winds, bring back
Adrian.

* *

Don't waste your time
laying traps for Lionel—

a raised eyebrow will do.

* *

If he doesn't come
in the next hour
it's all off.

& if he shows up
tomorrow . . .

what's a day lost?

James Mitchell

HOW TO BECOME A HERO OF HOMOSEXUALITY

1. Practice, practice, practice.
2. You are what you eat.
3. fell down from his thighs, revealing his handsome swollen member. "My God, Rodney," I cried, as he began with steady even strokes to
4. A tidy tool is a happy tool.
5. Know when to withdraw.
6. The man with the purple kneeband is coming.
7. The testes lie within the septate scrotum, are oval in shape and measure about two inches in length and one inch across.
8. No, thank you, not tonight.
9. Vaseline, please!
10. Aren't you going to take off your wristwatch?
11. Tell the lady at the Clap Clinic, "Well actually the trouble is you see I got an itchy whizzer."
12. No, thank you, not tonight.
13. Have you got a towel?
14. Tantric masturbation.
15. Retain an attitude of bemused superfluity.
16. Don't call unless you're serious.
17. Bathe daily.

[*Untitled*]

Jesse, I blew it at the baths!
There were all these guys prowling
around, with little white towels
over their asses. I said they
looked like giant diapered infants.
You said I had the mind of a poet.
In the steam room there were heavy
grunting noises. I couldn't see
anything at all. I walked down
the aisles past rows of cubicles,
doors slightly ajar. Inside each
a fat nude businessman sat, his
eyes gleaming with lust, spiderlike.
Suddenly you passed me, off to the
orgy room. I followed meekly.
There were more grunting noises
and a dozen naked fuckers at work
upon the pillows. It seemed to
me a writhing mass of protoplasm,
whose arms and legs undulated
like polyps in the sea. I broke
out laughing. I couldn't stop.
I put on my clothes and raced
from the building into the late
August sun.

THE ORGY

Stephen and Michael were already naked
on the floor, their genitals erect and
trembling. When Sebastian arrived, Martin
quickly released the prick from his pants

and slipped it into his mouth. Bill entered
Gerald from behind. Dennis, who was very
attractive, found himself with a cock
in his left hand, his right hand, in his
mouth and in his anus. Peter, excited by
the insistent presence of Walter's tongue
in his asshole, suddenly came in Allen's face.
Hibiscus and Tahara fell upon Scrumbly
and Sepulchra. Surprisingly, they all
came together. I myself made it with
Christopher. I fondled the swollen organ
out from his clothes and sucked it until
the milk of his penis flowed in my throat.
Many others were present. I've forgotten
their names. Their pale bodies squirmed
on the floor like libidinous trout in
a shallow stream.

I WANT TO SLEEP WITH TOSHIRO MIFUNE

and tremble at the thrust of his muscled cock bursting
up my ass

for I too am an unemployed samurai—vagrant, poor,
and very much without a lord; the only clan I belong to
is that of roaches, crawling around the kitchen floor

for I am a fairy mailman in San Francisco, but my
imagination is amazing, and exigent as Fuji

Toshiro, I'll meet you on the road to Edo; at sundown
we'll make samurai love in a deserted rice paddy

then, belting on our nemesis swords, together we'll
set forth into the world, and wipe out all the assholes
forever

James Nolan

JILALA

What happens when you cross
Jean Cocteau with a Miami housewife?

Jilala lounges with the funny papers
in green-face with an opium pipe.

Jilala serves hot blintzes from behind
a delicate belladonna spider's veil.

Jilala only in America Jilala
you ask me as you board the plane

what could ever lure you back
to California again.

Come now. Hybrids have no choice
but mid-air.

What do you think I'm doing here?

Harold Norse

LET ME LOVE YOU ALL AT STILLMAN'S GYM

freakshows. ferris wheels. rollercoasters. flash. flare. thrash.
surf. seasmell. saltair. youths in openair lockers. sand. sun.
nude bodies. they see me. in toilet window. make obscene
Italo hood gestures. up yours. *va fongool.* left hand pumping
bicep in crook of right arm. shame. I blush with shame. they
think I'm a girl! crimson shame. I'll die of shame. and delight.
excitement pumping hot blood thru my body. thick chestnut
hair over my eyes. red cheeks. ripe red lips. everybody looks
up at me. I peek over bathroom window ledge. *Hey! ya want
dis?* they yell laughing. mocking yet sweet. they grab their
dongs and wave and waggle them half-hard. their hips press
forward. *Come 'n' git it!* HAHAHA! my hair my skin like elec-
tricity. sparks shoot out of me. I grab the toilet paper cylinder.
slide it in. pull it out. they can't see. they make farting lip
sounds. the razz the Bronx cheer. *Hey kid wanna wop salami?
c'mon down!* they laugh. slap golden suntanned muscles.
gleam in openair showers. bending knees on sandy floorboards.
wet. hot. salty. sea and sperm. if the sandman brought me
dreams of you. I pick one out with my eyes. tall. lean. ample
cock. he looks up. defiant. provocative. tender. sneers like a
bully. slyly winks. buddies do not see this. secretly taps fore-
finger to breastbone. points to me. together. us. I'm breathing hard. suffocating. scared. tantalized. what shall I do? I
hide behind Auntie May's chintzy white toilet curtains. I think
I'd dream the whole night thru. I peer furtively over the ledge.
they have forgotten me. nobody looks up. I feel lost. they slap
each other's ass. grab at pricks. flick towels at balls. make
sexy gestures. yell hoarsely. then furtively look in my direction
from time to time. pretending not to notice me. bathing trunks
drying on sandy floorboards in the sun. I can almost smell the
musk from the trunks. they whistle between the teeth. sharp
piercing masculine. slap each other hard. smacking sound of

flat hard palms against flat hard bodies. whip towels across asses. grab balls. cackle. HAHAHAHA. shadowbox. they do not look up. I am forlorn. should I go downstairs? what will they do? call me dirty names and beat me up? the one I love looks up. loud Bronx cheer with puffed out lips. waggles cock contemptuously. sneers handsomely. lips curl arrogant and beautiful. for you brought a new kinda love to me-e—. I duck. I hide. crushed. rouged with shame and desire. in medicine cabinet mirror my face like a girl's. roses and olives in my cheeks. beautiful flash of brilliant teeth as I grind them in agonized frustration. Calcium they call me at school. Handsome Harry. pubic hairs thick black and shiny. come on little cat feet. I am 13. I watch the young men under the silk spray. twenty-eight young men bathe by the shore. they do not know who watches and loves them. behind the curtains I make love to America. in the closet I make love to America. my love is bigger than the Atlantic Ocean. America does not want my love. America throws sand in my eyes and tries to drown me in the Atlantic Ocean. but my love is bigger than any ocean. over the greatness of such space steps must be gentle. everywhere sand and waves and sun flashing. superb young acrobats in tank suits. they build a throne of bodies. along the sand I crawl on my belly to the throne. I am a slave to the monarch of flesh. no precious gems more precious than this throne of flesh. no god more precious than this throne of youth. let me love you all at Stillman's Gym. I am 13. I want to love America. America with its smell of gymnasiums and lockerrooms. America with its smell of hamburgers and hot dogs. America laughs at me. Steeplechase laughs. Luna Park laughs. the fat lady comes with jellyroll and laughs. The seal boy comes with black flippers and laughs. zip the pinhead comes and laughs. multitudes come on the beach and laugh. under the boardwalk the lovers laugh. the bank director in a beach cabana eats the newsie's shit and laughs. a great horseshoe crab rots on the sand with slimy maggots infesting its jurassic head and laughs. I poke it with a tarry stick. I dissolve into sea's endless rhythm. I fade out in relentless dumb seasure. I do not laugh.

fingers delicately palpate hairs on backs of thighs—
run gingerly along the bulge of buttocks

and rest gently on asshole—
please God I don't wanna do it!
stomach trembling—bands of young taut muscle ripple out
then suck in, waist tight—thighs arch like bows—
thick arrow ready from quivering tendons
to shoot—muscles straining—
I lower my head and grasp my feet—
tickle my toes with moist fingers
then bend down further—
straining—stretching—back and spine aching—
lips purse with kissy stress
towards the pearly glistening moisture—
heart pounding—tongue darting—bending forward—
hands clasped beneath thighs—locked—
grappling—pulling down—snout burrowing—
pressed in musky nest—aaahh! mmmmm!
GULP!

Venice, Calif., 1970

ISLAND OF GIGLIO

we sailed into the harbor
all the church bells rang
the main street on the crescent shore
hung iridescent silks from windows
stucco housefronts gleamed
rose, pistachio, peach
and a procession sang
behind a surpliced priest
carrying a burnished Christ
when I set foot on shore
a youth emerged from the crowd
barefoot and olive-skinned
and we climbed up rocky slopes
till dusk fell and close to the moon
at the mouth of a cave we made love
as the sea broke wild beneath the cliff

Rome, 1955

YOU MUST HAVE BEEN
A SENSATIONAL BABY

1
I love your eyebrows, said one.
the distribution of your bodyhair
is sensational. what teeth, said two.
your mouth is cocaine, said three.
your lips, said four, look like sexual organs.
they are, I said.
as I got older features thickened.
the body grew flabby. then
thin in the wrong places. they
all shut up or spoke about life.

2
a pair of muscular calves
drove me crazy today.
I studied their size, their shape,
their suntanned hairiness. I spoke
to the owner of them. are you
a dancer? I asked. oh no,
I was born with them, he said.
you must have been a sensational baby,
I said. he went back to his newspaper.
I went back to his calves.
he displayed them mercilessly.
he was absolutely heartless.
men stole secret looks at them.
women pretended he was a table.
they all had a pained expression.
he went on reading the Sports Page.
his thighs were even more cruel
thrust brutally from denim shorts.
the whole place trembled with lust.

San Francisco, 1973

TO MOHAMMED
AT THE CAFE CENTRAL

Tangier
sun and wind
strike the medina mosque

Mohammed
seventeen years old
puffs his kif pipe
sipping green mint tea
where blue phallic arches
rise among white walls
and berber rugs

the muezzin traces ALLAH
thru the moon's
loudspeaker
over casbah roofs
of Socco Chico

moneylenders
also sip mint tea
but Mohammed's eye
brilliant and black
darts among gray tourists
for a simpático friend
and glances at transistors
covetously
and tattooed mammas
you-youing
papoosed in laundrybags
peeping thru djellabas

the crescent sun plucks rugs
on lightning terraces
and dries
ten thousand years
in a second

Tangier/Paris, 1962

TO MOHAMMED ON OUR JOURNEYS

I was the tourist
el simpático
and your brother offered you
and also himself

I forgot about your brother
and we took a flat in the Marshan
with reed mats and one water tap
about a foot from the floor
and we smoked hasheesh
and ate well
and left for the south
Essaouira, Fez, Marrakech
and got to Taroudant
thru the mountains
and bought alabaster kif bowls
for a few dirhams and watched
the dancing boys in desert cafes
kissing old Arabs and sitting on their
laps, dancing with kohl eyes, and
heard the music down in Joujouka
in the hills under the stars
the ancient ceremony, Pan pipes
fierce in white moonlight
and the white walls with hooded figures
stoned on kif for eight nights
and the goatboy in a floppy hat
scared us, beating the air
with a stick, beating whoever came close,
Father of Skins, goat god,
and the flutes maddened us
and we slept together in huts

Venice, Calif., 1969

behind the glass wall
                          i see blue limbs
                          black fungus noses
    thighs kneecaps
                "i have the taste of the infinite"
ylem
        primordial squinch   the universe crushed into
                              a seed
nothing will satisfy me
            i write green ballets & hollow journeys
caught in the etheric web of yr crotch
            a hairy ocean of darkness

            dawamesc doors of pearl
            open to fiery radiance
majoun madness
        down marrakech alleys
    the   djemaa el fna
  squirming   with snakes
    in carbide glow

black gnaoua dancers!   lash sword!   flash teeth!
    under the barrow
      broiling in sleep   mouth
& nostrils buzzing with flies
                 genitals thick swollen out
    of big tear in pants
            derelict 14 year old street arab
      cameras   snapping
    like teeth/great souk
      swarms for dirhams

and who
    are you little arab
        i shared my visions
              and ate
      black hasheesh candy with
the doors of yr body   flung

open we twitched in spasms
muscular convulsions
heavenly epilepsy on the bed
in the hotel of the palms
prolonged orgasm
uncontrollable joy
of leaving the mind

Tangier/Paris, 1962

WE BUMPED OFF YOUR FRIEND THE POET

Based on a review by Cyril Connolly, Death in Granada, *on the last days of Garcia Lorca, The Sunday Times (London), May 20, 1973.*

We bumped off your friend the poet
with the big fat head this morning

We left him in a ditch
I fired 2 bullets into his ass
for being queer

I was one of the people
who went to get Lorca
and that's what I said to Rosales

My name is Ruiz Alonso
ex-typographer
Right-wing deputy
alive and kicking
Falangist to the end

Nobody bothers me
I got protection
the Guardia Civil are my friends

Because he was a poet
was he better than anyone else?

He was a goddam fag
and we were sick and tired
of fags in Granada

The black assassination squads
kept busy
liquidating professors
doctors lawyers students
like the good old days of the Inquisition!

General Queipo de Llano
had a favorite phrase
"Give him coffee, plenty of coffee!"

When Lorca was arrested
we asked the General what to do
"Give him coffee, plenty of coffee!"

So we took him out in the hills and shot him
I'd like to know what's wrong with that
he was a queer with Leftist leanings

Didn't he say
I don't believe in political frontiers?

Didn't he say
The capture of Granada in 1492
by Ferdinand and Isabella
was a disastrous event?

Didn't he call Granada *a wasteland*
peopled by the worst bourgeoisie in Spain?

a queer Communist poet!

General Franco owes me a medal
for putting 2 bullets up his ass

San Francisco, 1973

GREEN BALLET

> overhead
> on the bridge
trucks are speeding under angels

parks are empty & leaves are falling

> erect in mud
> their shoes slurping
on the riverbank two people
are breaking laws with their hips

at the top of the steps a sign reads

WORKERS ONLY   NO TRESPASSING

one is in rags
he is 16
he has red lips

the other is a man
who sees god as he looks up
> at the boy who looks down

the boy is thinking of the whore with the man
he spied on in the shadows
> by Hadrian's Tomb
as he clutches the man's ears
> tensing his thick
thighs
> & they come

the man thinks *god god*
> & the terror!
any moment all's reversed—
only the world's uniform THUD

all this time the Tiber sucking
> sucking
the fat mud

Rome, 1960

Frank O'Hara

HOTEL TRANSYLVANIE

Shall we win at love or shall we lose
                             can it be
that hurting and being hurt is a trick forcing the love
we want to appear, that the hurt is a card
and is it black? is it red? is it a paper, dry of tears
chevalier, change your expression! the wind is sweeping over
the gaming tables ruffling the cards / they are black and red
like a Futurist torture and how do you know it isn't always there
waiting while doubt is the father that has you kidnapped by
    friends.

      yet you will always live in a jealous society of accident
you will never know how beautiful you are or how beautiful
the other is, you will continue to refuse to die for yourself
you will continue to sing on trying to cheer everyone up
and they will know as they listen with excessive pleasure that
    you're dead
      and they will not mind that they have let you entertain
at the expense of the only thing you want in the world / you are
    amusing
as a game is amusing when someone is forced to lose as in a
    game I must

               oh *hotel,* you should be merely a bed
surrounded by walls where two souls meet and do nothing but
    breathe
breathe in breathe out fuse illuminate confuse *stick* dissemble
but not as cheaters at cards have something to win / you have
    only to be
as you are being, as you must be, as you always are, as you shall
    be forever
no matter what fate deals you or the imagination discards like a
    tyrant

as the drums descend and summon the hatchet over the
    tinselled realities

you know that I am not here to fool around, that I must win or
    die
I expect you to do everything because it is of no consequence/no
    duel
you must rig the deck you must make me win at whatever cost to
    the reputation
of the establishment/sublime moment of dishonest hope/I must
    win
for if the floods of tears arrive they will wash it all away
                                       and then
you will know what it is to want something, but you may not be
    allowed
to die as I have died, you may only be allowed to drift down-
    stream
to another body of inimical attractions for which you will
    substitute/distrust
and I will have had my revenge on the black bitch of my nature
    which you
                  love as I have never loved myself

but I hold on/I am lyrical to a fault/I do not despair being too
    foolish
where will you find me, projective verse, since I will be gone?
for six seconds of your beautiful face I will sell the hotel and
    commit
an uninteresting suicide in Louisiana where it will take them a
    long time
to know who I am/why I came there/what and why I am and
    made to happen

12/12/59

TO YOU

What is more beautiful than night
and someone in your arms
that's what we love about art
it seems to prefer us and stays

if the moon or a gasping candle
sheds a little light or even dark
you become a landscape in a landscape
with rocks and craggy mountains

and valleys full of sweaty ferns
breathing and lifting into the clouds
which have actually come low
as a blanket of aspirations' blue

for once not a melancholy color
because it is looking back at us
there's no need for vistas we are one
in the complicated foreground of space

the architects are most courageous
because it stands for all to see
and for a long time just as
the words "I'll always love you"

impulsively appear in the dark sky
and we are happy and stick by them
like a couple of painters in neon allowing
the light to glow there over the river

HOMOSEXUALITY

So we are taking off our masks, are we, and keeping
our mouths shut? as if we'd been pierced by a glance!

The song of an old cow is not more full of judgment
than the vapors which escape one's soul when one is sick;

so I pull the shadows around me like a puff
and crinkle my eyes as if at the most exquisite moment

of a very long opera, and then we are off!
without reproach and without hope that our delicate feet

will touch the earth again, let alone "very soon."
It is the law of my own voice I shall investigate.

I start like ice, my finger to my ear, my ear
to my heart, that proud cur at the garbage can

in the rain. It's wonderful to admire oneself
with complete candor, tallying up the merits of each

of the latrines. 14th Street is drunken and credulous,
53rd tried to tremble but is too at rest. The good

love a park and the inept a railway station,
and there are the divine ones who drag themselves up

and down the lengthening shadow of an Abyssinian head
in the dust, trailing their long elegant heels of hot air

crying to confuse the brave "It's a summer day,
and I want to be wanted more than anything else in the world."

Joe is restless and so am I, so restless.
Button's buddy lips frame "L G T TH O P?"
across the bar. "Yes!" I cry, for dancing's
my soul delight. (Feet! feet!) "Come on!"

Through the streets we skip like swallows.
Howard malingers. (Come on, Howard.) Ashes
malingers. (Come on, J.A.) Dick malingers.
(Come on, Dick.) Alvin darts ahead. (Wait up,
Alvin.) Jack, Earl and Someone don't come.

Down the dark stairs drifts the steaming cha-
cha-cha. Through the urine and smoke we charge
to the floor. Wrapped in Ashes' arms I glide.
(It's heaven!) Button lindys with me. (It's
heaven!) Joe's two-steps, too, are incredible,
and then a fast rhumba with Alvin, like skipping
on toothpicks. And the interminable intermissions,

we have them. Jack, Earl and Someone drift
guiltily in. "I knew they were gay
the minute I laid eyes on them!" screams John.
How ashamed they are of us! we hope.

Chuck Ortleb

THE HUSTLER

I like to walk
into a bar
where everybody
distrusts each other.
I know I'll leave the place
with a Triple A lover.

(We each have a penis shaped
for business and for fun.
In either case, you're shaped to
find someone.)

Depending on how much
you pay
I can swing up from the gutter
into the angelic lay.

And in cases of enormous
    cash in advance,
I can work up a sympathetic
        homo trance.

You pay, because
    some day
    I'll pay
for my fleeting New York City charms.

Oh yes, make money to my body,
make money to my long homeless arms.

SOME BOYS

When some boys
offer to dance
you can see how innocently
their cocks hang in their pants.
Pendulously, as they say,
connoting
horses, barns, liquor, hay.

Some boys open up their shirts
and the beauty almost hurts.

Some boys even undress in
rooms cluttered with Dylan on.

Some boys are evil.
They lure boys into deeper statements.
They take showers together
they eat flowers together
and call each other studs.

Some boys, though, do take to sex like apes and monsters and
    their fathers.
They get hair-raising erections.
Pools of smegma collect near their beds.
Discarded condoms build up in their backseats.
And dead pubic insects fall from their groins into
patches of vaseline.

The meat of rough alleys hangs in their underwear.
The kind of meat you pull out of the pants of muggers.
The meat in its American juice that lays in jeeps and B 42's
I mean the meat
of all soldier boys who will bomb the hell out of heaven,
the meat
of all those high school cadets
masturbating in the twilight as though they were landing a 747.

Stan Persky

SLAVES

Gay pride is the opposite of the slave fantasy
    homosexuals are given a parody of
    in the club that holds a slave auction or
    in the society that demands I have a slave
    mentality.
Politically simple: the half-hearted tolerance
    afforded by society-in-general cuts
    across and disguises the category of social
    class. We are taught to internalise it in an
    absence of community substituted for by the
    ghetto that gives us the imagination of
    owning a slave.
In a capitalist society where the slave class
    exists only as a metaphor the slaveowners
    want us to imagine we want to own slaves.
These owners of production and production-
    numbers never knowing that in history
We real slaves of the Greeks
Were mainly agricultural workers, textile
    producers, musicians, silver miners, history
    teachers, and poets.
Sometimes I think poetry is the benumbed and
    limited expression of the limited space
(a ghetto) we're given. Expressing real pain.
My master, also a slave, taught me this art.
Contrary to myth like the Greek slaves are contrary
    to Greek myth
Poetry isn't inspired-fuss like they say it is
    in school.
True, autobiography gets in the way
(For instance, I wanted this poem to express the pain
    I felt last night when you went off at midnight

not wanting me like you haven't wanted me
anytime but once and I beg, abject as a slave)
True, autobiography gets in the way
But now that I'm a master and slave myself, like
the crafty man who taught me, I don't believe,
as he did, that I'm simply the instrument
of a message that wants to get through
from a source we can't know
These messages come from the actual conditions of
slaves. I don't have pat answers to
explain the messages, like: gay pride, that
I transmit but don't autobiographically feel,
because I feel real pain.

August 21, 1973

SWANS

After lots of swans the summer dies.
The swans are here because they're part of the
stock and trade of poetry
And because this has something to do with someone
Who spent years wrestling them.
He taught me to write poems.
More sensible people wrestle angels
Which are imaginary or metaphors,
therefore different from swans who are
Real animals and often appear
as characters in cross-sexual myths
like Leda and The Swan
Angels and swans only get wrestled in people's imaginations
and have little to do with, say, the class structure
or homosexuality, as far as I can tell
Poets are real human animals resembling swans
or angels (whatever they are) or dancers
mimicking swans or those like me

A dying race of poets almost leaving themselves out
       of the political situation. Khmer Rouge
       encircling dancers on the verge of people's victory
       in Cambodia for instance. I'm in the working class
       or in some section or strata in a political situation
       that doesn't totally add up (neither do the years
       and poems)
But it's silly to imagine that poetry is outside
       of it. Which doesn't mean the swans
       disappear. Eventually it raises the question
       of revolutionaries and counter-revolutionaries.
Opposing capitalism, travelling swamis or poetry's
       stock and trade pretending not to be part of
       the class structure and Khmer Rouge encircling
       dancers etc. even though I don't really feel it
       right now and would rather dance with you
       in a bar and wish this poem were short enough
       to read to you inbetween drinks. Easy to choose
       not to be counter-revolutionary unless revolutionary
       is defined as metaphysically as angels or unless
       you pretend there are only swans, even though
       they are real animals and each of us
       has personal memories
The swans I've fallen in love with as opposed to you
       casually taking me in or leaving without me
After many a summer I'm tired of loving in cross-
       sexual myths.
I hear more puns in each line of poetry after years of it
       and the puns my body hears
After lots of swans the desire for swans dies.

August 29, 1973

Robert Peters

A CELEBRATION

you teach me
of that line
running

from the soft hollow
of the throat, down
the chest to the navel

losing itself
in hair. I follow it
with lips and tongue

along its warm
rib valley, turning
with it onto your

taut belly. I draw
your legs to my face,
bury there,

withdraw, my arms
push full-length
along your sides

from hip to armpit,
push, press:
halves into a whole

directed to
fractured light
exploding.

COOL ZEBRAS OF LIGHT

your fists
are warm
against my ribs

the musk of love
is hot mercury
pressed between
layers of skin.

at last
cool zebras of light
are feeding.

ON PUSHING A LOVER

we are wrestling.
soggy cartons, beech
leaves, dirt-powdered
sticks and stones . . .
my target is not only
the space between
your legs, or your
brown eyes, or your
taut neck as you thrust
against me in bed . . .
your angel waits:
release him! like
the body
love has its thunder.

ODE FOR JOHNNY RIO
================================

slight. biceps
like bullhide. bronze ribs
distinct. narrow waist,
a mist of hair
beginning at the navel. tight
shorts, thigh muscles trained
to look taut at glance-time,
all the time.

look mean, johnny.
the funny-scene won't end.

do it, iron butterfly!

some poor bastard
down on his knees
before you—every cell
a flame directed toward
your glans.

I write this with teeth
outside my mouth. you
are corrupting my lover.

LOVE AS PUSHER
================================

time as a ghost
robbed of its sheet:

a tourniquet
around your chest. below
at the beautiful junction
of cock and groin
impossible flowers burst

not needing stems buds
or leaves, form a direct
fire.
why can't this be forever?

I wait for a connection,
for hot bolts dropped
into place, searing.

TO LIVE IN THE SELF

to eat your
own cock
inside out

to tear at
the right ventricle
and the left

to do it fast,
forget to chew
right, swallow

whole, drink
throatfulls of bile
and piss

what it comes
down to is this:
it's a meal.

ON BEING RAVISHED
BY AN ANGEL

he fell through stars
through polluted air
to reach you sleeping.

you've wanted him to come
have kissed david's
ivory balls & wound
the figurine in silk, in
rituals of craving.

you saw him
on an english street
in a german pub, smiling
near a yucca in the west.
when he wakes you, and
you turn over moist
warm, surprised, let him
kiss you, let him rub
his hot celestial cock
against your groin, let
him drive it in—as slick
as steel, ravishing

and when he explodes
and floods your navel
know, love, that he'll
withdraw more easily
than he came, leave you
to recall the sound
of his wings beating
out of the room away
from the castle, on
to other hungry dreamers.

come into the next room.
I want to hold you.

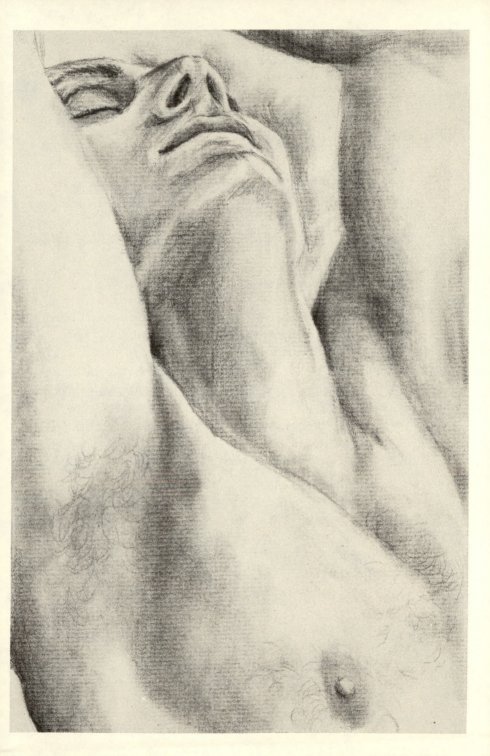

Drawing by Edward Aulerich

Vincent Sacardi

ODE TO A SUICIDE

PHOENIX, FIRE-RED, BURNING IN IMMUTABLE FLAME
DIFFUSING INTO INFINITY
MELDING INTO ELEMENTS OF TOTALITY
DIMENSIONAL-INEXORABLE-EPHEMERAL-IRREVOCABLE-
   ETERNAL

no more rain falling on my cheeks
no more warm sun
no more wind blowing in my face
no more crisp snow crunching under my steps
no more music
no more flowers

CRYSTAL FLAME, FIRE-RED, BLUE YELLOW GREEN ORANGE
STARK BLACK
ATOM, ELECTRON, MOLECULE, ELEMENT HURLED INTO
   DIMENSIONS
BURNING INTO THE COLOR SPECTRUM, THE FLAMING
   SUN OF INFINITY.

no more pain
no more bitterness
no more joy
no more laughter
no more sadness

MAN, HOW FRAIL A CREATURE THOU ART, IN THE
   WORLD OF INFINITY
MAN, HOW MAGNIFICENT YOU BE, IN YOUR DEFIANCE
   OF INFINITY
TRANSFERENCE, WHERE IS THY BURN?
. . . IN THE FLAMING SUN OF INFINITY . . .

in the caverns of the past:
  in the pale of promises not kept?
  in the laughs not laughed from the deep throat of life?
  in the pearls not sought after?
  in the prison of fear?
  in the smiles not returned?
  the songs not sung: GLORY GLORY HALLELUJAH . . .
  in the lost isolation of communication:
    in shunning warm and cold hands, not reaching out:
      in friendship
      in despair
      in need
      in asking
      in giving
      in getting
      in meeting
      in love
      in hatred
      in committing
      in expression

Ron Schreiber

PHANTASIES & FACTS

for Gary

phantasy: that people are isolated
pumas, roaming unexplored mountains
alone, each cat staking out its territory.
or mourning doves or swans
coupling in a canal, paired together,
content in that pairing.

fact: the sun is only one
configuration of a star. Orion
is another pattern, unexplored.

fact: my anxieties don't matter
this time. yesterday you worked
at the nursing home & went to school.
tomorrow you'll sleep with your friends.
& here you are.

                    pumas eat birds.
in winter their territories expand
& sometimes shrink. cubs commonly starve.

phantasy: that we can sleep with our friends,
our cats, our toucans.
                    fact: we can.

THE IMAGE OF YOU VIVID

for Nico

now that we're 3000 miles from each other   farther than ever
you seem vivid to me   smiling & relaxed   or doubled up in pain
frightened   your brown eyes   your face thin & drawn
when you're doing drugs instead of food
or flushed from the sun   red cheeks full

                                        now I'm away
I feel your nipples hardening   the wideness of your chest
your stomach almost fat but held in as you lie on your back in bed
or thin from all the tests the Amsterdam specialist took
your special diet   your fasting   your jumping away reflexively
not letting me touch you   or your cock full & hanging
no foreskin peeled back when you're soft   or hardening in my
   mouth
as I caress you   taste you   or like elastic ready to snap in two

the years we've been together blur into your shifting image
that I want to touch   even though I'd be afraid
if I were with you now   frightened of your fear
trying to hide my own   your body is more vivid to me
than my own body   just sitting across the room
or crying in Larry's apartment when your mother died
or spitting on me in our living room   or falling asleep
with the television on   or flirting   laughing   dancing
swimming in the Atlantic   wherever you're at   whoever you are

KAOSAN'S ROBE

for Kenneth Pitchford (Steven Dansky, John Knoebel)

i.

I collect the 17-year-old *dotera*
from H. Goren Cleansers. the old man
alone two years since his wife died,
listens to the Red Sox play the Astros
as he sews. reminding him of Florida
(I suggest), where he spent two weeks.
—have to keep your mind occupied, he says.

—a 60-year-old woman (I correct myself
remembering her youngest son was 10
—she just looked 60—her husband blind,
but operable if she could save enough money
for the operation, her oldest daughter
in a TB sanitorium in the hills);
—a 45-year-old woman made it for me.
(& two more, I could have said:
one for Faith, with red & yellow dots
in the fabric, matching her long hair;
one for Bill in blue stripes to match
his blue eyes). —an old woman made it for me,
I say. —it has sentimental value.

ii.

in the car we wait while you finish
writing your poem. Marjorie opens the gallery
for us men. sets up the chairs herself.

between acts of your reading I open the wine
but need someone to hold cups while I pour.
John declines, too busy selling *FF Journal,*
teaching us to learn to follow women's leads.
Karen holds the cups.

two of us gay men, one in rhinestones,
& Marjorie again, clean up afterwards.
we wait for you to finish talking
so Marjorie can get supper before the evening reading.

when we all drive back to your hotel,
there is talk & argument.
Steven bitches —is he boring you?
& you scream —it's *my* reading!
Karen sits nervous & angry, ignored
by men & their politics.

given the choice of following your effeminist
vanguard or remaining the Gay Enemy,
those of us who are learning to do drudgery
will choose Enemy of course. hopeful
as lesser enemies maybe to find useful service
in your kitchen when women come to power
with you as their voice to instruct us.

iii.

the agents who murdered Allende are the same men
who fuck their wives day after day
in kitchens, living rooms, one-room
nurseries/playpens/factories.

who screw the rest of us on battlefields
in streets & ghettos & whole countries
occupied by the stale blanketing greed
of America.

to listen means to listen,
not to talk. to make a revolution
means to work deep underground.
soft as the folds of the clean & mended
dotera I wrap around my body, hard
as the crust wrapped over the center of the earth.
fiery. waiting to erupt.

iv.

Kaosan's son must be a Japanese man.
maybe he works for Mitsubishi.
her husband may be dead by now.
maybe he could see before he died.

Faith left her husband to live in England,
returned to Berkeley. Bill is married.
he has three children, two daughters
& a son. H. Goren mends old garments,
listens to baseball games, vacations
in Florida once a year.

I wear the old robe. I listen & wait,
under the robe more naked than I am.
an old woman made the robe for me.
it has sentimental value.

1 / 3
___

not the marketplace   standing in line
beside barstools   along the promenade
in Brooklyn Heights   not wearing
just a towel in a bathhouse   a body
for perusal & use   not that auction
of clothes hairstyle crotchpadding cocksize

not merging spirits or contorted psyches
into a single butterfly acts of
consolidation of separate conglomerates
not ecstasy   the ascension
after ten months of Fridays

only this physical act   our bodies stripped
the act gratuitous   what there is to give
given without contract   two canvases
lightly brushed together in the night

Perry Scott

DICKE

That's it with the flag-signalling,
Dicke. Tonight I'll use sycamore
leaves.
     1 leaf means a Pierce-Arrow's passed
     our houses.
     2 leaves are for anguish
     3 for joy   if 4
     leaves show, run Dicke. If 4
        leaves show, run
               Dicke. Orange match-
        fire in my window means
           come over to share
        boyfur, the flower and its fuzz.
        My flag set's worn
           Dicke.
Some are lost, some rumpled in the wash. So,
        no more flag-
        signalling, Dicke.
        Tonight I'll use
      soft sycamore leaves.

Charley Shively

CARROTS FAREWELL

at 33 thousand feet
cumulus clouds
are walking into my life
   I could try
   buttermilk
Oh he has such
beautiful arms
they reach
pillow feathers
around his brim
   I can feel
   muscles ·in his leg
   against ,mine
   a communication
      Paul, are you listening
      I feel wave after wave
      coming to me now
      I do not hesitate
after a generation
some completeness
or is it just old age
he seemed more than pleased
I had waited
and not said a word
   finally it wasn't necessary
   was he so stoned
   he couldn't tell
   it was me?
or had I changed
during these years
of being ready
   only one person

could anwer
and he wasn't talking
as he zippered up
we held each other
kissed and left
just another
Breezewood exit

CONTINENTAL DRIFT

lap into lap
lips every
swaying towel
surfacing skin
hallway to mirror
lamp to moth
halfway toes teeth
gristle folded
in mathematical
mouths of rivers
liberation runs
libidinously melds
mellow grass
in halfhallways
skin covering
prepuce diction
kissed away in
soft sucks of
undertow swimming
waters, talons
teeth spaced
two by four
oral fitted
stones in fixtures
snores in silence.

FOR STEVE JONAS:
FOUR YEARS GONE GREEN

bitter root knots
sunk in pine
cut nails
        of stealers
        muggers killers
        all over these streets
they say wading
in your life
                Beacon Hill
                Esplanade
                South End
        trailing all ways
                from Georgia
                entrails
tin horn lovers
playboy physiques
gone Steve Reeves
        better
        in reverse bitterness
                blond taunting
                indifference

he left before
i was ready
ivory lungs
play games below
your belt
        blood sliced
        neat in cans
        spread over hands
        a smear as sure
        as leaky Cowper's glands
you cant help notice
Lindall Place
a hippie palace
on an edge

trimmed with thread

precarious

how you could rail
against sentimentality

fences in these leaves
we passed on sidewalks
alone poets
buzz along
most of our wishes
otherwise realized
machete voices
pissing absinthe puss

I walk on your sharp bones
catching in my throat

IMMEDIATELY

immediately
his nipples rose
his moustache shone
his eyes opened
his thigh tightened
his hair cut loose
his pants were down
his penis purple
he groped me
we formed rings
making semen
in kazoo mud.

SNOW POEM

snow tasting fresh
from the body
salt mingled sex
celebration of black bark
trees
northeaster naked
genital heat melting
minds kissed with tongues
body troughed limbs
crest
wrapped with one another's
exposed parts
wet with one another
in light orgasm

Aaron Shurin

EXORCISM OF THE STRAIGHT/MAN/DEMON

You are just the kind of man
    who has always   sucked me
into loving him.   The kind
unable
to feed me love back.

You stuff me   with your need
and say it is my need.   You stick
    your hardness in my face
        and say it is my softness.
It IS my softness.   Go away.
I have no more openings
for hardness.

Straight man in me   who I never wanted.
Power spoon-fed me   that I despise.
        to lord over
      to judge   and not listen
    to thrust, not pull
    to be hard   and never   yield.
Look out!   I expel you.

And warn you not to   shove yourself
into the hands of my mouth.
See how hard your cock is?
That's how strong my jaw is.
    That's how fierce my heart is   and my love.

    My hate is not
from angry love   but from anger.
Not for who you are   but how you treat me.
Filling my need to be loved
    with your own need   to conquer love.

Man   Man   I call your name
in throwing you out.

     And reclaim my formlessness.
     And re-interpret my desires.
     And receive the world as made for me.

Spirit!   I bend to you.
     I cross / I bow
I deny the demon   and cry for his expulsion:

Obaob   Abniob   Baiax   Ousiri

                Spirit
who is alive in me   witness
this casting away.
The old threats   are leaving me.
I am living.

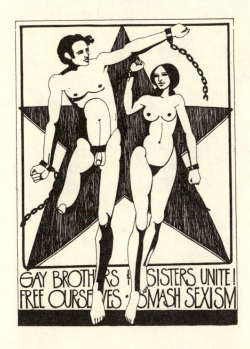

Drawing by Bruce Reifel

David Emerson Smith

From L STREET

I. L Street Elite

Put signs up in all the showers
for heteros only/start a chapter of
the QKK (Queer Klux Klan)/put Black hoods
over our heads/wanting head/instead
sucking mind cocks hanging under the solarium
conversation of Freddie Greenfield's cock
and ball jabber/old man's naked stare and
nervous twisting tongue/irritated at audacious
comments on L Street pricks through hot rocks
hanging in each ear and eye and thigh and
between the legs of beds and arms of chairs
and so many cocks/balls/and snuggly pubic
bare boys in societal brassiere/asking for
your shampoo instead of your sensual/ness
rack of meat you so neatly hide neath pants/
the up and down and empty sound of empty
parking lot budweiser beercan and school boycott/
hungry for their missing spiritual/ity deleted
by their fading heroes and heroines/deodorant/
band roll on like wasted toiletfuck imagery/
and the blonde lovely bearded/hung man/holding/
conference with youngish poet dreams/weaning him
to feel me/hand on knee and under the
brutal balls and crotch of the empty pack
of fools that forgot which end went down/
and how we get around and the sound of
rapid breathing/
exhumed

II. L Street Expose

                    i
              saw more
              cock and b
              alls in ten m
          inutes than most
          people see in five
          years of baths bars
          and locker room YMCA
          heyday swaying to and
          fro to the tune of ste
          amroom blues little p
            ointed ones big bulb
              ous ones   anciently
                  sag   ging ones
                                hanging th
                                ere like
                                liver on
                                a butcher
                                rack love
                                ly long un
                                circumcise
                                ·d pricks
                                popping in
                                veins like
                                plumbing
                                day dream
                                drains and
                                pubescent
                                newly etch
                                ed tool ha
                                lf hard wi
                            th coming of
                            age in ameri
                                cas waste
                                landfuck
                                    ing

Jack Spicer

A PRAYER FOR PVT. GRAHAM MACKINTOSH
ON HALLOWEEN

Infernal warlocks dressed in pink
And children wearing masks by night,
Protect my friend from sundry harms
And rest his body in your arms.

Ghosts of eternal silences
And pumpkinfaces wreathed in flame,
Consume the military flesh
Of those who borrow young men's lives.

You white-faced boys who trick or treat
And ring the doorbells of the dead,
Twist out each patriotic bone
Of those who consummate the loan.

And have the nasty little girls
Who steal the seed from dead men's loins
Make peepee on their uniforms
And dance on their conscripted flag.

Avenge for him this Hallowseve
Each moment of captivity.
Let every ghost of liberty
Parade before him in his sleep.

Infernal warlocks dressed in pink
And children wearing masks by night,
Protect my friend from sundry harm
And rest his body in your arms.

for A. J.

> *"Let shadows be furnished with genitals."*

He was reaching for a world I can still remember. Sweet
and painful. It is a world without magic and without god.
His ocean is different from my ocean, his moon is different
from my moon, his love (oh, God, the loss) is different from
my love.

In his world roads go somewhere and you walk with someone
whose hand you can hold. I remember. In my world roads only
go up or down and you're lucky if you can hold on to the road
or even know that it is there.

He never heard spirits whispering or saw Aphrodite come
out of the water or was frightened by the ghost of something
crucified. His world had clouds in it and he loved Indian
names and carried some of his poems in a pouch around his neck.
He had no need of death.

Rimbaud without wings.

Forgive me, Walt Whitman, you whose fine mouth had
sucked the cock of the heart of the country for fifty years. You
did not ever understand cruelty. It was that that severed
your world from me, fouled your moon and your ocean, threw me
out of your bearded paradise. The comrade you are walking
with suddenly twists your hand off, the ghost-bird suddenly
leaves a large sea-gull dropping in your eye, you are sucking
the cock of a heart that has clap.

Calamus cannot exist in the presence of cruelty. Not
merely human cruelty, but the cruelty of shadows, the cruelty
of spirits. Calamus is like Oz. One needs, after one has
left it, to find some magic belt to cross its Deadly Desert,
some cat to entice one into its mirror. There Walt is, crying
like some great sea bird from the Emerald Palace, crying,
"Calamus, Calamus." And there one is, at the other side of
the desert, hearing Walt but seeing that impossible shadow,

those shimmering heat waves across the sky. And one needs
no Virgil, but an Alice, a Dorothy, a Washington horse-car
conductor, to lead one over that shimmering hell, that cruelty.

So when I dreamed of Calamus, as I often did when I touched
you or put my hand upon your hand, it was not as of a possible
world, but as a lost paradise. A land my father Adam drove me
out of with the whip of knowledge. In the best sense of the
word—a fairy story. This is what I think about Calamus.
That is what I think about you.

Boston, Mass.
February 1955 ?

CENTRAL PARK WEST

Along the walks the sweet queens walk their dogs
And dream of love and diamonds as they pass
And I could be a statue or a stone
As they walk by me dreaming of their gods.
Beside their path, an apple's throw away,
I see that old erotic garden where
Our parents breathed the wasteful, loving air
Before the angry gardener changed his will.
The park has no room for that memory.
Its paths are twisted like a scattered sky
Of foreign stars. The spinning queens go by
within their orbits, leaving me alone.
What cosmic joy. The last companion here
Is Priapus, the gardener's ugly son
Who crouches in the bushes with his shears
And hasn't got the hots for anyone.

FIVE WORDS FOR JOE DUNN
ON HIS 22ND BIRTHDAY

I shall give you five words for your birthday.

The first is *anthropos*
Who celebrates birthdays.
He is withered and tough and blind, babbler
Of old wars and dead beauty.
He is there for the calmness of your heart as the days race
And the wars are lost and the roses wither.
No enemy can strike you that he has not defeated.
No beauty can die in your heart that he will not remember.

The second word is *andros*
Who is proud of his gender,
Wears it like a gamecock, erects it
Through the midnight of time
Like a birthday candle.
He will give you wisdom like a Fool
Hidden in the loins
Crying out against the inelegance
Of all that is not sacred.

The third word is *eros*
Who will cling to you every birthnight
Bringing your heart substance.
Whomever you touch will love you,
Will feel the cling of His touch upon you
Like sunlight scattered over an ancient mirror.

The fourth word is *thanatos,* the black belly
That eats birthdays.
I do not give you *thanatos.* I bring you a word to call Him
Thanatos, devourer of young men, heart-biter, bone-licker.
Look He slinks away when you name Him.
Name Him! *Thanatos.*

The last word is *agape,*
The dancer that puts birthdays in motion.
She is there to lead words.
Counter to everything, She makes words
Circle around Her. Words dance.
See them. *Anthropos* ageless,
Andros made virgin, *Eros* unmirrored
Thanatos devoured.
Agape, Agape, ring-mistress,
Love
That comes from beyond birthdays,
That makes poetry
And moves stars.

[*Untitled*]

We find the body difficult to speak,
The face too hard to hear through.
We find that eyes in kissing stammer
And that heaving groins
Babble like idiots.
Sex is an ache of mouth. The squeak
Our bodies make
When they rub mouths against each other
Trying to talk.
Like silent little children we embrace
Aching together.
And love is emptiness of ear. As cure
We put a face against our ear
And listen to it as we would a shell,
Soothed by its roar.
We find the body difficult and speak
Across its walls like strangers.

[*Untitled*]

For you I would build a whole new
        universe but you obviously find it
        cheaper to rent one.   Eurydice did
        too.   She went back to hell unsure
        of what kind of other house Orpheus
        would build.   "I call it death-in-
        life and life-in-death."   Shot
In the back by an arrow, President Kennedy
        seemed to stiffen for a moment before
        he assumed his place in history.   Eros
Do that.
I gave you my imaginary hand and you give
        me your imaginary hand and we walk
        together (in imagination) over the earthly ground.

CHAPTER IV OF
"A FAKE NOVEL ABOUT THE LIFE
OF ARTHUR RIMBAUD"

They said he was nineteen; he had been kissed
So many times his face was frozen closed.
His eyes would watch the lovers walking past
His lips would sing and nothing else would move.

We grownups at the bar would watch him sing.
Christ, it was funny with what childish grace
He sang our blues for us; his frozen lips
Would lift and sing our blues out song for song.

Intemperance of heart and of the mind
Will block their progress to the last abyss
Unwinkingly; they listen to the wind
And find a final ceiling in the throat.

ORPHEUS' SONG TO APOLLO

You, Apollo,
Have yoked your horse
To the wrong sun.
You have picked the wrong flower.
Breaking a branch of impossible
Greenstemmed hyacinth
You have found thorns and postulated a rose.
Sometimes we were almost like lovers
(As the sun almost touches the earth at sunset)
But,
At touch,
The horse lept like an ax
Into another orbit of roses, roses.
Perhaps
If the moon were made of cold green cheese,
I could call you Diana.
Perhaps,
If a knife could peel that rosy rind
It would find you virgin as a star,
Too hot to move.
Nevertheless,
This is almost goodbye.
You,
Fool Apollo,
Stick
Your extra roses somewhere where they'll keep.
I like your aspiration
But the sky's too deep
For fornication.

George Stanley

TOUCHING

If I eat dust, and, am proud of it,
nostrils to the wind,
                              if a flame
to no-god-at-all burns
at the center of me—
                              more,
is kept shrined there,
                              if there is
no shade in me,

shadow, nook, arbor
where to escape
a hobbyist's justice,
I will leave what-I-am,
find a place in the packedness,
jostle him I know not
on the bus, like naked
on the beach, touching on all sides
flesh I know not, trembling—

Touching.

Force me not
up against
the body
of my beloved,
blind, babbling
against his heart,
racked by dry sobs
to hide from
                    a casual meeting
with him.

Richard Tagett

WITH HEAD LAYING ON SOFT COCK

The Inbetween
Mind thinks
best · Love
& Filosofy
Comfort
a Good Shit
/ Jackoff
Aperitif /
. Come now to
The Inbetween
where my
legs come together
and there
are drawers full of
paper
to look at
with eyes
closed / dreaming
Pirates, Brothels,
Geraniums,
Head laying
on Soft Cock
well spent
delight,
think .

Dear Alfred Charles Kinsey:

I have no more expectations of life
Than the gall wasp, Sequoya,
Or flagpoles in the plaza. Or
Stone I could be / stone / I could
Be electrically / chemically with
Or without the penis / head some en-
Joi. Who call themselves men. Or male.
Who are. And who are stone as well.

> *I am over thirty*
> *and under the sun*
> *my mother is dead*
> *my father ellipses*
> *in rectangles he*
> *erects for my brother:*
> > *husband of fat ankles*

Dear Alfred Charles Kinsey,
Do you have a foot fetish too?
Is there a pendulum clock
In your anteroom? Has dissecting
Led you to this, a study
Through pessimistic glass?
How positive are you? Surely
You remove the seeds
When you squeeze the orange.

I have
  no expectations; I have
  dreams. I dream dreams,
  and I live dreams,
        simultaneously.

I believe
That windows are made for looking from,
That what lies beyond
Is part of me. And what is part of me
Lies beyond.
It's a seed-spent path
between,
and I a fertile agent yet
no more than that,
no more,
no less than dream.

(*cc: Sigmund Freud*)

9/70

WANT

want
nothing
more than to be
heard

touched   is it?
at last let's fuck
want   what's wanted

the object is these boys   their
touching
games

you know
don't you   what they
want

nothing
more than to be
consumed.

I WANT TO LIVE
IN VIEW
OF THOSE MOMENTS THAT BE LIFE JOINING
THE HEART WITH MIND
TO REMAIN
THE CHILD IN VIEW
OF THE SUN THE SEA THE MOON
TO TALK
WITH THE BREEZE
TO GO
ON & IN
INSIDE
THE CRAWLING   WINGING
ONE WITH ONE WITH ALL.

+

I WANT TO MOVE
CHANGE   CONTINUE
REMAIN AT ONCE
THE SONG THE SINGER
THE EAR OF MY NEIGHBOR
THE BITE THE BUG
THE SORE OF HIM WHO'S ME
THE SOAKT LAUGHING LAUGH OF HIM WHO'S ME FLYING
LAGOONS THE PLACES NAMED
FOR US BY US OUR
CLOCKT TONGUES WE
NEED & WISH
THE TOUCH UPON   COMMINGLING
IN THE HARDWOOD
NETTLEBED OUR
LOSS
BETWEEN THE YELLOW HEAT
THE WHITE COLD
HABITAT OF LOVE-FUCK HAD
IN THIRSTEN RIVERS OF MOUTH

MINE THAT IS YOU IS YOURS ONE
SPECK BREATHING
THE FROTHT SEA FORTH

AH! STREAMING THIGHS   NECK
NIPPLE   CHEEK
GLINT-LIT FUCK!

come
come to be go   going
on . . .

+

I WANT TO SEE   TO FEEL
THE LIMIT OF DAY
THE INDESCRIBABLE BLUE
GREEN
THE PINK
LIMIT OF ROD
LIGHTNING NIGHT
TO DASH
INTO THE BEAM
LISTEN
ONE WARM EAR
CURLED UPON
ERUPTION MOUNTAIN OF YOU
WHO'S BODY
THE GROWING PEAKS
SING SILENCE NO-SONG OF ALL SONGS SUNG
INSIDE
THE SILKEN AMPLE HAIR OF YOU
TOUCHING   TOUCHING   TEACHING
ALL
ALMOST TOO PERFECT
CRYSTALLITES SCREAMING
BAWL-LIFE
BALLING ON . . .

come
come to be

WHO DOUSES WITH CHERRY LIFE
RED-HOT WHIMPERING IN GOLDEN ARMS!

+

BUT IF I CAN'T BE
WHAT I WANT TO BE
WITH YOU
IT'S NOT OURS
OR ANY UNEARTHLING'S FAULT
FOR OTHER SONGS
SOME SWEETER   SOME LESS
PERMEATE THIS AIR
& AFTER-SCENT.
BE & BE WITH ME EVEN WITHOUT ME
IS ALL
I ASK   IS ALL
I KNOW IS WHAT FORMS THE WHOLE
THE NOTES THE MOMENT RESTS
CLEFS
OF WINGING ONES & SLURS
CRESCENDOS
UNIMAGINABLE EVERYWHERE.

Hunce Voelcker

EARTH, Part 3

His naked innocence assumes the air
His youth and age become the water's steam
And as the redwoods breathe, his fog grey hair
Wraps round my neck beside his rippled stream.
He is air, fog, steam, mist, smoke, whims of wind
Bemused seed spreading sprite, bejewled boy
Part Planet's plants produce, bathe, breathing him,
His whims with sun and sea shape earth, and toy
Just as the redwoods' breath adds oxygen,
And as the oceans move, he brushes hair,
And as he is essential to the fire's grin
I with all beings living breathe his air.
I naked stand on sculptured hill to be
His lover, living as he enters me.

GREAT SPIRIT, Part 2

Come sit beside me by this mountain stream,
Take off your clothes, we swim here when we wish
As nature we can love each other dream
And dream into our spirits as our kiss
Of mind of soul of Spirit on our eyes
Can realize. Merged karma of our grin
By our merged bodies loving is implied . . .
Together until end, begin, begin.
Begin (as we have joined) this breathing tree,
This breathing earth's evolving consciousness,
This air, this mountain rock, sun, moon, this Sea
These breathing beings: love's felt eagerness
As grass and acid are our sacraments
As all of life, through spirit, complements.

John Wieners

IMPASSE

Is it enough my feet blackend
    from streets of the city?
My hands coarsend, lovely limbs
    bone to dust.

Is it enough? my heart hardend
arms thickend eyes dim.
Is it enough I lost sight of him
Ages ago and still follow after
        on some blind, dumb path?

Is this aftermath? Am I ever
to follow that, always
The same man, one dream
to death, only another
Dream one never wakes from.

Cities stretch eternal streets
lead on. Star-points of light
flicker over the harbor. Oceans
beckon. I cover the waterfront
who have been near no docks.

They are too lonely.
There is no audience watching there
through the night
to reflect one's own face
passing in a glass.

It is eternal audience
and my feet hardend, my heart
blackend, nodding and
bowing before it.

ACT 2

I took love home with me,
we fixed in the night to
sink into a stinging flash.

¼ grain of love
    we had,
2 men on a cot, silk
cover and green cloth
over the lamp,
    the music was just right.
I blew him like a symphony.
  It floated and
    he took me
down the street to
    leave me here.
3 AM. No sign.

  only a moving van
    up Van Ness Avenue.

Foster's never like this.

I'll walk home, up the
    same hills we
      came down.
He'll never come back,
    there'll be no horse
      tomorrow nor pot
tonight to smoke till dawn.

He's gone and taken
my morphine with him
Oh Johnny. Women in
  the night moan yr. name

          6.19.59

A POEM FOR
THE OLD MAN

God love you
    Dana my lover
lost in the horde
on this Friday night
500 men are moving up
& down from the bath
room to the bar
Remove this desire
from the man I love.
Who has opened
    the savagery
of the sea to me.

See to it that
his wants are filled
on California Street
Bestow on him lar-
gesse that allows him
peace in his loins.

Leave him not
to the moths.
Make him out a lion
so that all who see him
hero worship his
thick chest as I did
moving my mouth
over his back bringing
our hearts to heights
I never hike over
    anymore.

Let blond hair
burn on the back of his
neck, let no ache
screw his face
up in pain, his soul
    is so hooked.

Not heroin
Rather fix these
hundred men as his
lovers & lift him
with the enormous bale
of their desire.

Strip from him
hunger and the hungry
ones who eat in the night.
The needy & the new
found ones who would weight him down.
Weight him w/ pride and—
pushing the love I put
    in his eyes.

Overflow the 500 with it
Strike them dumb,
on their knees, let them
bow down before it,
this dumb human
who has become
    my beloved
who picked me up
at 18 & put love
so that my pockets
will never be empty,
cherished as they are
against the inside flesh
    of his leg.

I occupy that space
as the boys around me
choke out desire and
drive us both back
home in the hands
    of strangers

6.20.58

BALLADE

This poem is in tribute to Jack Spicer because he wept over it.

Alice O'Brien
would he care or be crying
over the way we're carrying on tonight?
would it matter,
his feet dancing I imagine.

We worked for a while together, I hated him
he was 30—yet Mabel the pianist he bought drinks for
and washed off her keyboard.

I am sick on the taste of my tongue.

She will cry, colored Mabel,
not many others, his ex-wife—
his dead girl, he said
She's dead, thank God.
And a good lover—8 yrs—died in the war,
(later, I learned in a riot near Roxbury Crossing)
who asked him to take off my glasses, he told me,
to punch both my eyes,
let's see how you look without those goggles
on wham one eye wham
the other; His mother—good enough for you!
when the lover dragged Alice down her three flights of stairs
back home after Alice left over
the black eyes—You should'ah stayed with him!

Just a queen, but he was 20
one night for a minute
a cheap bum in pegpants and wingdcollar
(sang every time he came up to the place)
Lord above me make him love me
the way he should,
and Alice loved him, I guess,

as much as—smiled anyway—later drank a double
That's Right! a double rye! one
gulp when the bum left him for Fitchburg.

Help Alice O'Brien hung himself

in Charles Street jail
from his shoelaces.

Would it matter in his black cell
the queen of the
In his French heels, I said
honey you'll fall
off that ladder

           changing the redlight bulbs
           dancing in them—cleaning up our tables

           very gay in front of the bar
           eyes squinted he swished to
           what was his song—
           I got it bad and that ain't good.

           We all hated the four eyed runt.

Tears on his face?
I have never seen a hung man.
Their eyes bulge out and their tongue
sticks from a blue face.

Ah Alice ironic
(from shoelaces)
           sequin ones for Halloween.
But I remember now he always wore loafers for dancing.
           No laces.

We heard later the police
           broke his neck by mistake I see
Alice O'Brien hung
head down on
his gay world, swinging
under the yellow lights.
Prescott Townsend comes tomorrow to the burying
   of Alice O'Brien.

We are all of us lost, Lawrence said.
No difference to Alice
if Alice knew and went
dancing instead of dying
off the laces
of his high French shoes.

               November 1955

THE OLD MAN:

All about the sexual urge strikes in the night,
lover moves to beloved, mouth closes upon mouth.
Nowhere do the lonely stand long, unattended.
In dark rooms, cocks bulge against trousers.
A dull image, to the sexually uninitiated.

But to me now, came memories of what men call lust,
that excuse allowed them to press up together moments.
Call it desire. No, more than that. In need
Of oblivion from time, to possess and be possessed.
I know no other cause. Loneliness calls through the house

like a curse, but falls on deaf ears. Locked here
blind by poverty, my disease to seek out on some dark highway
That lover who will release me into heaven. Dim respite
which ends when his arms let me go. If even that. No arms
exist for me, but those locked in doors.
In other arms, in love with me, but still sharing
Other arms for ecstasy.

                                    Holy saturday

IN LOVE

A simple song
to long for home and him
lounging there under the moon.
What is he? Who is my heart
he should mean this much to me?

Is it sex, or grass stains on your shirt?
night, or sight of flesh
lying on its side in the Pine Grove?

Groove of memory, overgrown with weed
                    and speedballs,

barren trees, or summer garden,
hate and blood, or flood of seed
                    from ardent partner?

Who can say, what declares care
demands desire
for his hands through your hair,
the sudden flight of birds
that brings him home despite dim stars.

CONTEMPLATION

Why do they turn away from us
on the streets when we love
them. Billie Holliday was the story
of my whole life & still is

                    on sunlit Sunday afternoon

opposite the elevated railroad

                    tracks

at Cambridge street & Charles
when every hope burns to stinking incontinence,

the winter wind blows sand & sea off countless holiday
extravaganzas, between body & soul

Sultry California boulevards proliferate upon a shredded
mortality, as the abyss of former promenades wells

                    to fecundate interiorly
                        again at Land's

End.

        The pleasures of young escapades envelops
        smoked glass store-fronts outside the empty Scotch & soda
                                        orders
Bar.

Imaginary Interview in the style of Beckett Malanga. Seen through the eyes of Simone de Beauvoir as an imaginary interviewer of Greta Garbo, a.k.a. Gusta:

GG: Madame Simone, I suppose you wonder why I've asked you here this afternoon. It's because I was reading, and impressed with your photograph, that I came across while rifling through a closet shelf of news clippings, I wondered if you (knowing I'd be thrilled) care to interview after I discarded such personal trivia. [*Nostalgically*]: The ire of former times has abated in the direction of a certain Ms. Mary Theresa, *tu reconnais, n'est-ce-pas?*

SdeB: I concern myself most assuredly, in forgoing prior lucidities.

GG: Gracious, then you accept an assignment in debating the earlier merits and acerbities in the direction of another laxity?

SdeB: I can't say I do, but I persevere in attacking the general miasma, mythically winnowing through the debasements in our governmental genetic cabinets, as demeaning athwart the titular habiliments of feminine costume. That intrigues me, just *where* did that rubbish buy lent out of your files? I mean, it's corpuscular, leaning pieces of O'Leary plastic.

GG: That's a good one. I didn't know, are you Irish, through the Mulligan and the Moose.

SdeB: No matter. A missing link, as morning becomes Electra. No mind to the proper names.

GG: Knowing an assumed fraternity, could you guess Odin refers to Intrusion? or Celt to Cornish.

SdeB: Please, let's get down to basics.
How much do you weigh?
You've put on weight. And your earlier efforts

GG: Appear in vain, approximate unavoidably majority acclaim; mildly awarded. A generous sampling in taste.

SdeB: Decorum being sensible adjunct, to a sumptuous surveillance. You continued your efforts in the film, tracing antecedent lives from post-modern authorities, in genres of geographical locales and constabularies, *à la* Romany *and* South America.

GG: No, I dare say not. I've haven't budged an inch; as a chatelaine to Victor P. Immanuel.

SdeB: Goodness, gracious, pungency betrays berating gestating twilight's aura. A glimpse at our reunion in the art of letters gently. There can never be enough of a good thing. A just cause. A noble . . .

GG: Intrusion.

SdeB: At your request, of course, in the word of the unconscious sharply risen through old words, and straight kept sentences in the ancient field of honorable.

GG: ALWAYS, darling monde. Theoretical correspondents called caught hept in proselytizing to the fickle mouths of impertinent men. I can see there's no such disdainful distaste culled imaginatively other mindfully.

SdeB: You read somewhere . . .
Chelsea, Grammercy, Sardinia?

GG: None of *trompe l'oeil*.

SdeB: In Boston last week.

GG: In regards, yesterevening your spring-pilgrimage to Massabeille, about Our Lady of Lourdes.

SdeB: Doubly.
   Acceptance of A P P A R I T I O N A U T O M A T I C A L L Y A t t r i b u t e d intrigues seduction. Ariadne either acquits fatally reversed exotic miscreants both rurally benefitting Prescott; desperately staunching the body and blood of Her Son, for the supreme act of sacrifice, heard daily in the weekly celebration of the Mass, not upon the federal apronstrings braided as coils from Circe's turret Pike's peak.
   I consider poetry and problematic philosophy to be *outré* ga u c h e, avowed, regarded skitterish tabulating of worldliness galoshed Southern central juxtaposition to this N o r d de P A R I S visitation, mourned you professionally servant girls upon the M A S O N N A E D by-paths of myput-out. P O I N T E D ingly, p l U r a l l y.

GG: Coquettishly.

SdeB: How dare you? [*Stammering*]: Ruefully. Those were my assumed tears you heard. Bled lachrimae trinkles from Parisian judgmented plazerias. [*Both laugh musically and discuss sidereal asides in delightful, sundry mirths of gratuitously acquired innuendos.*] I gather you've seen a good deal of the United States, through a friend of yours, with whom you are severing three decades of codification. Is he too strange as in the example of H.P.L.

GG: I dunno. It's gone beyond.

SdeB: Desire? A long, as usual awkward pause, generated by the unmentioned escort reimburses the tacking of these relations. S O B E R, harried and T-continent.

GG: Fruitlessly

SdeB: You've been too kind, over simplification aligns aspersion, a good jostling now and again never hurts any one. I receive first hand you've gone shopping incessantly around Town in two years of all the things bought, which do you favor? Or prefer? Consider post-operation four . . .

GG: Automobiles, Tens, a Sunny afternoon, hostess.

HOW TO COPE WITH THIS?

A mean, dark man
was my lover
in a mean dark room
for an evening

till dawn came
we hugged and kissed
ever since, first and last
I have missed

him, his mean, dark ways.
Mean, dark days
are upon me in the sunlight
even yet, I fear his foot

feel his cock and know it
as my own, my sown
seeds to reap
when the full neap

of pleasure falls, his kiss
reminds me, our dance
in the dark, my hope
and only scope.

TWO YEARS LATER

The hollow eyes of shock remain
Electric sockets burnt out in the
skull.

The beauty of men never disappears
But drives a blue car through the
stars.

Jonathan Williams

LEXINGTON NOCTURNE

don't you?
don't you want to?

a gentleman doesn't ask young men
questions like that;
he probably begins with reveries on the French word
tendresse
and how much better it is than our own

tendresse
what you find in the Adagio
of Rachmaninov's *E Minor Symphony,*
after the Largo, which was so
rapacious
and full of longing . . .

sacred *longing;*
to be long, to *belong* to the company of those
who trust the holiness of the heart's affections . . .

and to be *long gone*
up the first road to Eros,
as prone to the emotions as Sebastian,
full of his arrows . . .

back to the gentleman
and the young man:

Lexington, Kentucky,
the boy sharing the double-bed is called _____,
from Texas,
full of *tendresse* . . .

22, old enough to ask,
as I did rhetorically, above:

do you?
do you want to?

the truth is
I never said a word . . .
I burned
and merely remembered what
Tram Combs used to say:
NEVER FUCK YOUR FRIENDS! never
let a tablespoon of come
come between friends . . .

one of those nights
with eyes open all night
(even they sweat),
but by 3 o'clock my foot and calf
relax,
the mind lies back
in the light of the white room,
where it waits for you
to shift your body
freely
in deep sleep . . .

by 6 o'clock the light brightens,
and if I move carefully
I can move the spread just a little, see
your back where the t-shirt's pulled up
and the top of your thigh shows

and look at you
and wonder what any of this would mean to you—
This meaning the *lust* to hold you
and bring you
into the Brotherhood of Lovers . . .

the very first thing to say, the fact is
it is most seemly, most apposite, most circumspect for men
to fuck boys—
"men are men's joy"

if I were a Dorian nobleman
I would explain to _____, as I slipped it in,
this is not just semen up your ass,
this is *class*, this is arete, this is how
you learn to be a man

but this is 2500 years post Plato,
who fucked everybody up

thus I see you as your eyes open in the Lexington dawn
and put my hand in your hair and
let it hang
just an instant
there
and let that be all
for then

"men are men's joy"
means what it says

in another town
on another night

Eros, that sore, three-time loser,
shall strike again,
old friend:

do you?
do you want to?

man
to
boy

"HOW DO YOU GET IT ALL OUT?"

King Onan's Way
is one way

a dulcimer attached to a nervous sytem
using a felt pen is a (more discrete) way

●

yet *melos* is hot, sticky mess—
remember how Jack Spicer got as
purple as a stiff prick,
discharging the Lyric Frenzy
into the cruddy audience

●

Paul Goodman's
right as rain:

"the more you come,
the more you can"—

you can't go to the pump
too often!

●

"I detest and I lust!"

O Great Catullus,
with you!

in the world,
up to the hilt

THE APOCRYPHAL, ORACULAR
YEAH-SAYINGS OF THE ERSATZ
MAE WEST

(1)   Mae West, to God:

It's the only show in town!

(2)   Mae West, to W.C. Fields:

I've got the posse, sheriff, if you've got the time.

(3)   Mae West, to Charles Ives:

Use what's lyin' around the house, daddy,
and let it all hang out.

(4)   Mae West, to a dwarf:

Honey, you ain't seen nuthin' yet!

(5)   Mae West, to Sappho:

My real name is Terra-Belle Incognita, doll.
I'll bet you never discovered a whole continent before . . .
Say, baby, if you had arms 3000 miles long
this country would be too tired to get out of bed.

(6)   Mae West, to Colonel Sanders:

Linger-fickin' beats chicken-pluckin' any time!

(7)   Mae West, to a heckler:

If your cock's as big as your mouth, honey,
I'll see you after the show.

(8)   Mae West, to Li-Po:

Put that thing in a canoe and come on down the river!

(9)   Mae West, to J. Edgar Hoover:

A hard man is good to find.

(10)   Mae West, to the Masked Bandito:

Is that a gun in your pocket, or, do you love me?

(11)   Mae West, to Ezra Pound:

An ounce of erection is worth a pound of allure.

(12) Mae West, to Jean Genet:

Chicken ain't nuthin' but a bird—
you do it your way, I'll do it mine.

THE HONEY LAMB

the boysick (by gadzooks thunderstruck)
Rex Zeus, sex
expert, erects
a couple temples
                    and cruises the Trojan Coast . . .

eagle-eyed, spies,
swoops,
swishes into town

ponders, whether 'tis nobler
to bullshit, brown
or go down
on
      that catamite cat, Kid Ganymedes,
                              mead-mover,

erstwhile eagle-scout
bed-mate

MODERN LOVE LYRIC
("HE PROMISED ME LOVE
BUT GAVE ME NINE INCHES"),
FROM THE PAGES OF JIZ COMIX

strange

to be praised in a poem
for sporting
a ten inch cock

after years of lascivious observation
I'd calculated I had eight and a half
and you had nine

love in bloom
makes the sights
worth seeing

for instance,
how nice
to recognize your own asshole,
to see it striding over a hill
dressed in green taffeta
in your lover's dream
for the first time

love in bloom
makes the sights
worth seeing

Terence Winch

THE JUNGLE

Q. What is the jungle like?

A. The jungle is like an interview about the jungle. It is like a big gray dog in the lobby. The dog has hands like a man's. But there is no hair on them. The jungle began when the high school teacher with the broken foot opened his door and fucked his two cutest students till their ears flew off. They were not able to reach an orgasm unless he whispered to them "I will fuck you till your ears fly off." The students returned with three six packs. They all went to the party. When my amazing radio sailboat love died, you could fuck a bird in the hot mud. You got me so confused. I started to lie. I started to shut up. You could fry this chicken in the jungle.

Q. Why do you always ignore me at parties?

A. You do not try to make me feel good when we are together. I keep feeling it going through me. Frank Sinatra's mystical participation in the crucifiction. In the jungle, people got little flappy ears like Walt Disney characters and they walk real funny. In the jungle, the concept of perfection is used freely. They say, "What a perfect idiot." I laid all the eggs in the refrigerator. I thought Buster Keaton was a second-rate Scottish boxer. You ran across the street to your home. Your father sucks his fish. I said to my brother looking at you, "I sure would like to fuck him." My brother didn't say anything. I apologize for my nephew. You smell like gasoline. I was a good uncle. I was too tense to dance.

Q. What is your concept of affirmation and negation?

A. When you are infectious, do it quickly into the night. But if you have washed yourself clean with the tiny hands of your proteges, discharge slowly once every six years.

Ian Young

SKY / EYES

On Earth,
as I rested my fingers on your hands,
how often my eyes would look into yours,
and how much we could tell
from the colours of eyes:
Brown eyes are solid, unbluffable,
strong and unchanging . . .
Dark blue eyes look forward,
to words and action spilled in a moment . . .
Green eyes like mine are cautious, intuitive,
like a cat's, and slightly sinister . . .
Grey eyes are sad—
quiet, and strangely appealing.
Then, there are those light blue eyes—
Adriatic or Arctic—clear and cool,
honest, and infinitely gentle;
eyes of the child, the innocent,
open to the ideal, and the winter.
Looking into them,
you could see the sky,
cloudless, fresh and bright.
Your eyes were like that . . .
Here,
it is so quiet
as I fly.

A SUGAR-CANDY BIRD

In bed
with my friend's young brother,
a boy of sixteen:
his penis
swelled
so big and thick
I thought it would
                          split
like a ripe pod,
or those glazed
and gaudy candy-birds
from Mexico—
                          break
suddenly open,
and spill
white sugar dust
over us both.

THE SKULL

When the boy undressed,
I saw on his left shoulder
a blue tattoo—
two daggers, crossed
under a skull.
'That's pretty phony,'
he said, and laughed,
uncertain.
Later, I half expected it
to peel off
in my mouth.

ANGEL

Three thirty at night:
our city room
silent and dark . . .

I lie in bed
watching Rick,
his body just now smooth against mine,
now crouching, naked, by the window,
leaning,
motionless,
in the black air.
One arm draws back the curtain,
the other
rests upon the sill . . .

I watch him there a moment—
slim and light in all that darkness,
then look beyond him
to the lighted street outside . . .

Still coldness
gives the air
substance.
A few blurry lights—
yellowblobs, and white,
(without my glasses).
A car passes—
tires on the wet road—
the steady, dying sound . . .

As if all Night were stopped
at this one moment—
I in bed,
Rick at the window,
cold street waiting.
Across the road,
the EVANGEL TEMPLE's neon sign
goes off and on.

Part of it's broken. The rest
gives us a message,
glowing
ANGEL.
ANGEL.
ANGEL.
ANGEL.

COLOSSUS OF RHODES

Colossus of Rhodes
standing astride the harbour
to honour the sun-god
(till the earthquake toppled it)—
less impressive than Chris
(a sun-god himself)
in his blue denim
standing astride nothing.

He
won't come to bed but
smiles his sly smile
as I unzip his fly,
kneel, and proceed to
blow my head off.

My colossus
is a little weak in the knees.
Yes,
one day, he'll topple too.

TWO MOTHS FOR RICHARD

Rick Asleep

your naked chest
breathing

nipples

corks bobbing

on a hot sweet sea

Rick-rider

astride your back

your shoulderblades
made for wings

where will you carry me

EPPING

I kissed a boy in a wood

some green moths
darted in the sun

another bit of magic

CHINESE BOY, 14

an orange

      just
      neatly
      opened.
Taste

JAPANESE BOY

knives

a dragonfly
sliced
on a silver dish.

Biographical Notes

HECTOR TITO ALVAREZ (*New York City*)

Born 1952 in New York City of Puerto Rican parents. Educated at Erasmus Hall High School, Brooklyn, and Franconia College, N.H. (visual arts). Taught at Adams School, N.Y. "Came out" May 1974. Is a painter and has had several small shows, including one at the Instituto de Cultura in San Juan, P.R. His poems have appeared in *Franconia Review* and *Fag Rag*.

WILLIAM BARBER (*San Francisco*)

"I was born in 1946 and grew up outside Boston, near Longfellow's Wayside Inn, but came to San Francisco in 1965 to attend S.F. State, Languages/Writing/-Drama/Dance/Music/Art. I have published over the past ten years numerous poems, stories and five comic porno novels (as Billy Farout). *Abyss*, a collection of my poems, with commentaries by friends, was published in 1974. I support my writing by lecturing guided tours of San Francisco."

BRUCE BOONE (*Berkeley, Calif.*)

Born 1941. His poetry has appeared in *Sebastian Quill, Panjandrum Journal,* and elsewhere. His long poem *Karate Flower* was published in a chapbook by Hoddy-poll Press, 1973.

VICTOR BORSA (*San Francisco*)

"Born in Saskatchewan, Canada, 1931. Attended teacher's college in Saskatoon; taught school for four years. Switched to engineering drafting at which he is still employed in San Francisco. Started writing poetry at age 16, published in various journals in Canada and U.S. Two books out: *Untangle the Wind* (1967) and *A Search For The Wild* (Fiddlehead Poetry Books, New Brunswick, 1971). Also has had half a dozen poems read over Canadian Broadcasting Corporation's network radio program *Anthology.*

JOE BRAINARD (*New York City*)

"Born in Salem, Arkansas, in 1942. Grew up in Tulsa, Oklahoma. Moved to N.Y.C. after high school. Early cartoons with poets for *The East Village Other, Other Scenes,* etc. Editor of *C* Comics: more cartoon collaborations with poets. Much book and small literary magazine covers and illustrations. As a writer: 12 books out. As a painter: 15 one-man shows. Currently showing at The Fischbach Gallery, and painting Soho roof tops out window of new loft." Books include: *Bolinas Journal; Selected Writings; New Work;* and *I Remember* (Full Court Press, 1975).

PERRY BRASS (*New York City*)

Born in 1947 in Savannah, Georgia. "At 27 I find myself feeling alone now; still writing poetry and painting and trying to deal with the renewed vacuity of this country, the splintering and destruction of the Gay Liberation Movement and the personal experience of growing up again in New York. Some of this experience is getting deeper into the things that please me most—poetry, art and music—after living in the whirlwind of the aborted political struggles of the late 60's and early 70's." Poetry has appeared in *Gay Sunshine, Mouth of the Dragon,* and elsewhere.

ADRIAN BROOKS (San Francisco)

"Born 1947. Is a poet, journalist and performing artist. He has lived in Mexico, Europe, Africa, India and Nepal and has been part of underground art and political movements in the USA and abroad. Currently he lives in San Francisco where he is working with a free theatre company and helping Harold Norse with *Bastard Angel*. He is also working on his first book of poetry." His poems have appeared in *Gay Sunshine* and *Fag Rag*.

IRA COHEN (Kathmandu, Nepal)

"Born 1935 in NYC. Lived for four years in Tangier, Morocco, where I edited *Gnaoua*. Further alchemical studies in NYC where I practiced spirit photography. See my film, *The Invasion of Thunderbolt Pagoda,* an opium dream in three parts, as example of astral drama and practical divination. Also produced film of Living Theatre's *Paradise Now* in Amerika for Universal Mutant. Produced *Hashish Cookbook* by Panama Rose, the Great Society & Jilala, a record of Dervish music (Morocco). Now operating as *Starstreams* for *Bardo Matrix* in Kathmandu, Nepal, where *Seven Marvels*, a collection of poems, has just been published. A wanderer on the path, I seek the perfect stranger in Love & Poetry."

KIRBY CONGDON (Brooklyn, N.Y.)

Has published five collections of poems: *Iron Ark; Juggernaut; A Key West Rebus; Dream Work;* and *Black Sun* (Pilot Press, 1973). His most recent chapbook is *Shirt Poem* (1974). Has published the avant-garde literary publication *Magazine*. "I took over Jay Socin's Interim Books series around 1966, and have continued with it as money permits. I make a living as a typesetter for a computer, but save what energy I can for working with the underground/avant-garde people in poetry, helping out with Ralph Simmons' Cycle Press, doing some painting and music writing and collecting books; I put my own poetry before everything else."

ED COX (Washington, D.C.)

"Born 1946 in Washington D.C. Catholic schools & when graduated from high school worked as apprentice printer for two years & then went into Navy; two years in Japan & two years in Baltimore; did GI organizing after discharge & then returned to D.C. to work at GI coffeehouse; worked part-time as typist until almost two years ago when started working as secretary for government & am part of group wanting to have a gay community center & I want poetry to be a part of my life." His book of poems, *Blocks,* was published by Some Of Us Press (1972).

EMILIO CUBEIRO (New York City)

"Born in NYC in 1947. He writes plays, produces them and sometimes acts. His main interest and work is poetry and the performance of it. He currently is working with a band, Emilio Cubeiro & Edwin Kapinos & the Freek Band. He suggests you see them perform sometime."

TIM DLUGOS (Washington, D.C.)

"Born 1950, Springfield, Mass. Early life spent in Western Massachusetts and Northern Virginia. One year as a novice in the Christian Brothers; then college at LaSalle in Philadelphia (1969-73—the beginning of my Wonder Years). First collection: *High There* (Some Of Us Press, 1973)."

ROBERT DUNCAN (San Francisco)

Born 1919 in Oakland, California. Has published many volumes of poetry and his poems have appeared in hundreds of literary magazines. He was deeply involved in the "San Francisco Renaissance" of the 1950's. Since 1951 he has lived with the painter Jess Collins. His poetry has been influenced by Pound, Gertrude

Stein, William Carlos Williams, Charles Olson, Jack Spicer, and others. He writes: "I make poetry as other men make war or make love or make states or make revolutions: to exercise my faculties at large."

DAVID EBERLY (Boston)

"Born in 1947 in Boston where he still lives and works. His poems have appeared in several gay papers and magazines, as well as in *Hanging Loose*. He is presently at work on a pamphlet of poems, his first."

JIM EGGELING (San Antonio, Texas)

"40, paiderast, poet, painter, is currently preparing two volumes of poems for press. Published in *Hearse, Suntan, Fag Rag, Gay Sunshine;* anthologized in *The Male Muse*. He collects beautiful boys, has a B.A. in English and an M.Ed. He is a Gnostic priest and the Executive Director of Forward Foundation, Inc. He makes his living at the Texas Employment Commission."

KENWARD ELMSLIE (New York City)

Born 1929 in NYC. Raised in Colorado Springs and educated at Harvard. Six volumes of his poetry have been published: *Pavilions; Power Plant Poems; Album; The Champ; Circus Nerves;* and *Motor Disturbance* (1971 Frank O'Hara Award for Poetry). He collaborated with Joe Brainard on *The Baby Book* (1965) and several subsequent volumes. He has written several opera librettos, including *The Sweet Bye and Bye, Lizzie Borden,* and *Miss Julie*. His musical theatre piece *The Grass Harp,* based on the novel by Truman Capote, music by Claibe Richardson, has been recorded. His recent novel, *The Orchid Stories*, received critical acclaim.

R. DANIEL EVANS (Philadelphia)

Born 1944. "I've been very active in the Philadelphia poetry scene for the past five years. Some of my poems appeared in the anthology *Hellcoal Annual* and in chapbook *Snort* (1973). My work has been printed in most of the major gay literary publications and elsewhere. Co-edit *The Painted Bride Quarterly* with Louise Simons and have run the poetry readings at the Painted Bride Art Center for the past six years. I've given readings at colleges, bookstores, art galleries and libraries. Am a member of the GAA and Gay Academic Union. Also teach art history at a two-year college in Philadelphia."

GERALD L. FABIAN (Washington, D.C.)

"Born 1924, Chicago, Illinois. Infancy spent with miner immigrant grandparents in Butte, Montana. To Calif. in 1930 with mother who had re-married. To U.C. Berkeley, 1941. Active duty USNR 1942–45. Return to Berkeley 1946—sent down 1948. Menial jobs all through 1950's, struggle against alcoholism; by 1960 had mastered himself well enough to re-enter Berkeley and get a degree. Life in North Beach put him in close contact with many important figures of the 'renaissance.' Became an active poet and translator only after 1966. Now living in D.C. where he teaches, translates and produces one or two poems a year." Poetry chapbook: *Odissea Finita* (1969).

SALVATORE FARINELLA (Boston)

"Born 1940 in Hartford, Ct. My poems have appeared in over 50 magazines. First book *Hunger* (1972), a special issue of *Road Apple Review*. New book: *The Orange Telephone,* Boston Good Gay Poets, 1975. I have read my poems on both coasts of the U.S. Am an editor of *Fag Rag* and *Sun Tan,* a literary magazine. Poetry for me is a method of thinking. I believe almost any experience can be made universal but universality is not the key. If a poet is writing about sex in johns or sucking cock or fucking boys, the poem through its music can be descriptive and transform what the 'straight' world believes to be permissive promiscuity into a moment of ephemeral beauty. Poetry is where you keep your head."

EDWARD FIELD (*New York City*)

Born in NYC in 1924 and still lives there. His first book of poems, *Stand Up, Friend, With Me* (Grove Press), won the Lamont Award. Other books: *Variety Photoplays* (Grove); and *Eskimo Songs and Stories* (Delacorte). He wrote the narration for the documentary film *To Be Alive*, which won an Academy Award. Gives poetry readings around the country and teaches poetry workshops. Has read at the Library of Congress.

CHARLES HENRI FORD (*Kathmandu, Nepal; and Crete*)

Born in Mississippi in 1913. Before he was 20 he had published his poetry in a dozen literary magazines and was editing one of his own, *Blues: A Magazine of New Rhythms*. In 1933 he collaborated with Parker Tyler on the Gay novel *The Young and the Evil*. His books of poetry: *The Garden of Disorder* (1938); *The Overturned Lake; Sleep in a Nest of Flames; Spare Parts; Silver Flower Coo;* and his selected poems, *Flag of Ecstasy* (1972). During the war he edited the surrealist magazine *View*, where many young American poets were first published. He also turned his talents to painting, photography, and filmmaking (*Johnny Minotaur*, 1971). Was lover of the Russian/American modernist painter Pavel Tchelitchew (1897-1957) for 23 years. In-depth interview in *Gay Sunshine* No. 24 (Spring 1975).

JAMES GIANCARLO (*a.k.a. Maya Desnuda*) (*San Francisco*)

"Born October 1947, I have followed a mercurial path through form, image & word to find myself now here, in my own body, exploding in vulcanic dance. I am caught by what sparkles beneath the surface. I want to see it & show it." Currently involved in San Francisco gay theatre groups under the name Maya Desnuda. His poetry has appeared in *Gay Sunshine* and *Manroot*.

ALLEN GINSBERG (*Cherry Valley, N.Y.*)

Born in Paterson, N.J., in 1926, the son of Naomi Ginsberg, Russian emigre, and Louis, a lyric poet and schoolteacher. He was an important part of the San Francisco Renaissance/Beat Movement of the 1950's. Since that time he has traveled around the world, participating in readings and festivals, often accompanied by his long-time lover, Peter Orlovsky. His books include: *Howl* (1956); *Kaddish; Reality Sandwiches; Planet News; The Fall of America; Airplane Dreams; Gates of Wrath; Empty Mirror; Iron Horse; Ankor Wat*. The famous *Gay Sunshine* Interview with Ginsberg (Issue No. 16, 1973) has been reprinted in book form.

JOHN GIORNO (*New York City*)

Born in NYC in 1936. He is founder of Giorno Poetry Systems which sponsored the Dial-A-Poem series (Museum of Modern Art, NYC; Philadelphia Museum; etc.) and has published several records of contemporary poets reading their own work (about twenty poets per record). He was involved in the movie *September on Jessore Road* with Allen Ginsberg (1971). Is deeply into tantric Buddhism. Books of poems: *American Book of the Dead; Poems; Balling Buddha; Cancer In My Left Ball* (1973); *Subduing Demons in America* (1975). Has been published in six anthologies. See in-depth interview in *Gay Sunshine* No. 24 (Spring 1975).

ROBERT GLUCK (*San Francisco*)

"I'm 28. I live in San Francisco & have two books out: *Andy,* a book-length narrative poem (1973), and *Marsha Poems,* a chapbook. Born in Cleveland, moved to L.A., then Scotland, then Berkeley, then New York, then San Francisco. B.A. Berkeley, M.A. San Francisco State; received Browning & Academy of American Poets Awards. Some things I think: any metaphor can be a plot (esp. of transformation), people and things are portrayed truer if shown in relation to others. I like the poems of mine selected for this anthology, with their long clear lines, out in space and sexual like the naked arm of a biker as he signals a left hand turn."

PAUL GOODMAN (1911-1972)

Born in NYC. Ph.D. in humanities from Univ. of Chicago. His many books include fiction, poetry, drama, education, social criticism, and studies in psychotherapy, linguistics, sociology, religion, and city planning. He was a frequent speaker at conferences on peace action, libertarianism, education, and other community concerns. His poems were gathered together in the posthumous volume *Collected Poems* (Random House, 1974). He described himself as a "conservative anarchist." Was bisexual throughout his life.

STEVE JONAS (1927-1970)

"Stephen Robert Jonas Jones was raised in Atlantean Georgia, attended Boston Universities. He worked in the U.S. Armored Services, studied under officers of U.S. Dept. of Army. Armory history includes among these offices: *Love, the Poem, the Sea & Other Pieces Examined by Steve Jonas (for Michael Farmer, USN)* (White Rabbit Press, S.F., 1956); *Transmutations* (Ferry Press, London, 1968); *Selected Poems* (Stone Soup Press, Boston, 1973). He also became involved in racial insurrectionists' compositions. Temptations to earlier condemnations, among these, towards godly anarchism, staunch witless assumptions. His experiences of a hereafter took place upon the dinner time of the second month in the first year of this decade (1970); his final resting place is Mt. Hope Cemetery, Jamaica Plain, Mass." [Bio note by John Wieners, April 1975.] See critical essay on Jonas' poetry in *Fag Rag/Gay Sunshine,* Summer 1974, p. 19.

E. A. LACEY (*South America and Canada*)

E. A. Lacey's book of poems, *The Forms of Loss* (Toronto, 1965), was the first Canadian book to deal openly with Gay themes. His most recent book, *Path of Snow,* was published in 1974 by Ahasuerus Press.

MICHAEL LALLY (*New York City*)

"Born Orange NJ in 1942. Considered myself 'straight' till 1972 and first successful sex with a male. Since then share sex and sensuality and much else with all kinds of people, making the term 'bi-sexual' seem too limited implying as it does only two kinds of people. I have written as a 'straight' person, as a 'gay' person and as a confused person with occasional moments of clarity when it all makes brilliant sense. See *Rocky Dies Yellow* (poems) and *Catch My Breath* (prose) (1975). I have edited an anthology, *None of the Above,* due out in 1976, and publish a series of chapbooks under the imprint O Press."

GERRIT LANSING (*Annapolis, Md., and Ft. Lauderdale, Fla.*)

"Born Albany, N.Y., 1928, grew up on farm in Ohio, B.A. Harvard, M.A. Columbia, worked for publishers in NYC as well as varied temporary jobs. For those interested in starry symbolism, of strongly Neptunian character, Sun in Pisces, Scorpio rising." Poetry has appeared in various literary mags as well as in anthology *A Controversy of Poets* (Doubleday Anchor, 1965). An enlarged edition of his book *The Heavenly Tree* was published in 1975.

WINSTON LEYLAND (*San Francisco*)

"Born in Lancashire, England, in 1940 and came to the U.S. at the age of 12 with my parents. College studies: Philosophy, Theology (M.A. equivalent); and Medieval History at UCLA (M.A., 1970). I was ordained Catholic priest by Cardinal Cushing in 1966 but left the structured church two years later because of the Church's position on Vietnam, ecclesiastical fascism in general & my own increasing radicalism. Have been Gay movement activist & editor of *Gay Sunshine* since early 1971. Will edit an anthology of Gay literary interviews in 1976. Influences: Teilhard de Chardin, Daniel Berrigan, John Wieners. Am socialist pacifist."

GERARD MALANGA (*New York City*)
"Born in 1943 and grew up in NYC. He attended the University of Cincinnati and studied with Richard Eberhart. In the 60's he worked seven years with Andy Warhol. He has published 17 books and chapbooks of poetry, among them: *Screen Tests/A Diary* (in collaboration with Andy Warhol); *The Last Benedetta Poems; 10 Poems for 10 Poets; chic death; Poetry On Film;* and *Incarnations: Poems 1965-1971.* He has two books forthcoming: *Lines for Penelope Singer* and *Rosebud.* He is currently poetry editor of *The Translatlantic Review.*" See interview, *Gay Sunshine* No. 20 (January 1974).

PAUL MARIAH (*San Francisco*)
Born in 1937. Co-editor of *Manroot* poetry magazine and publisher of Manroot Books. His poetry has appeared internationally in literary publications. Has written and lectured on the oppression of prisoners in American penal institutions. His poetry chapbooks include: *Personae Non Gratae; Love Poems to an Army Deserter Who Is in Jail; The Spoon Ring; Six Imaginary Letters of Young Caesar on the Bythenian Tour, 81 B.C.; Letter to Robert Duncan While Bending the Bow.* His work has also appeared in several anthologies.

WAYNE McNEILL (*Toronto, Canada*)
"I was born in 1953 in Toronto and raised there. I attended the University of Toronto for a short time & quit to concentrate on writing. A thin volume of my poems, *Shells,* was published by Ian Young's Catalyst Press when I was nineteen. It is a classic of adolescent confusion, chaos & arrogance. A year later a second volume, *Pantomime,* was published through Catalyst. In this book I was much more tender towards boys. I've had work printed in various magazines & periodicals in Canada."

TAYLOR MEAD (*New York City*)
He has been involved in many underground films since 1960, mainly in Gay camp roles. He started out as a child-man-hero in Ron Rice's Beat Generation film, *The Flower Thief.* During the later 60's he starred in several Andy Warhol films, most notably *Lonesome Cowboys* (1969). He has written three volumes of a diary, a mixture of aphorisms and poetry: *Anonymous Diary of a New York Youth,* vol. 1, 1961; vol. 2, 1962; and vol. 3, 1968, under the title *On Amphetamine and in Europe.* See the interview in *Gay Sunshine* No. 25 (Summer 1975).

TOM MEYER (*Yorkshire, England; and Highlands, N.C.*)
"Born St. Valentine's, 1947, Seattle, Washington. Spends his time with Jonathan Williams, living part of the year in Cumbria, England. He attended Bard College & has two books of poems in print: *The Bang Book* (1971) and *The Umbrella of Aesculapius* (1975), both published by The Jargon Society."

JAMES MITCHELL (*San Francisco*)
"Born 1940 in Hartford, Connecticut. Graduated 1961 from Boston Univ., then six years of post-graduate studies in Europe. For a time he lived in the Haight-Ashbury, engrossed in numerous delusions. At 33 he became a Zen student and a newspaper boy, attaining distinction as neither. Lately employed at the San Francisco Welfare Department, where his incompetence generates much confusion. Has been urged to stop writing poetry by everyone who knows him." Editor of *Sebastian Quill* (1970-72). Publishes poetry chapbooks under the imprint of Hoddypoll Press. His own books include *Tales of Sagittarius; New Poems* (1974); and *Buddhist Poems* (1975).

JAMES NOLAN (*San Francisco and South America*)
Born in New Orleans in 1947 to a French creole and Irish family long established

in the French Quarter, where he grew up, interested first in painting and then in writing. His first book of poems, *Why I Live In The Forest,* was published in 1974 by Wesleyan University Press.

HAROLD NORSE (San Francisco)

Born in NYC in 1916. MA degree from New York University. He left the U.S. in 1953 and spent fifteen years abroad—in Europe and North Africa; returned to the U.S. in 1968. His books include: *The Undersea Mountain* (1953); *The Roman Sonnets of G. G. Belli* (translations and adaptations);*The Dancing Beasts; Karma Circuit; Penguin Modern Poets 13;* and *Hotel Nirvana,* Selected Poems 1953-1973 (City Lights, 1974). His poems have appeared in numerous magazines internationally and have been translated into several languages. He currently edits the literary magazine *Bastard Angel* and is preparing a volume of his memoirs. See in-depth interview in *Gay Sunshine* No. 18 (July 1973).

FRANK O'HARA (1926-1966)

Born in Baltimore, Md. In Navy, 1944-46. At Harvard Univ. (B.A.), then at Univ. of Michigan (M.A.). Lived in NYC 1951-66. He worked for *Art News* and the Museum of Modern Art. He died in a freak accident at Fire Island. Frank O'Hara had several books of poetry published during his lifetime. All of them (together with previously unpublished poems) were gathered together in *The Collected Poems of Frank O'Hara* (Knopf, N.Y. 1971).

CHUCK ORTLEB (New York City)

"Born on what is now called 'Christopher St. Day' in 1950. He is the oldest of ten children and was raised in New Jersey, Missouri, Minnesota and Kansas. He attended the University of Kansas where he taught for a year. He has worked for Hallmark Cards and the Coordinating Council of Literary Magazines. He is currently an account executive at an advertising agency in NYC." His poems have appeared in *Mouth of the Dragon* and other literary magazines.

STAN PERSKY (Vancouver, B.C.)

"Born 1941, Chicago, into working class family with petit-bourgeois aspirations; being gay became part of consciousness age 14 in love with Mel Weisberg; first friendly help in writing age 16 from Allen Ginsberg; 1958-61 US Navy (Europe); 1961-66 San Francisco, lived with Robin Blaser, worked as warehouseman and bartender, poetic mentor was Jack Spicer, beginning of politicization during Vietnam demo; 1966-present, Vancouver B.C., went to school at Univ. of B.C., continuing political commitment to student/gay/communal/socialist struggles, lived with Brian DeBeck several years, currently working at Mental Patients Assn., write for *Western Voice,* a newspaper of working class struggle, in men's c.r. group, friends with George Stanley, Lanny Beckman, Tom Sandborn; books: *The Day; Slaves* (New Star Books, 1974)."

ROBERT PETERS (Huntington Beach, Calif.)

"Born on a farm in Wisconsin, 1924. Ph.D. in Victorian literature, Univ. of Wisconsin. Has published books on A. C. Swinburne and John Addington Symonds. He is best known as a poet and has published a dozen books of poems; among them: *Songs for a Son; The Sow's Head and Other Poems; Cool Zebras of Light* (1974); and *The Gift To Be Simple* (1975). He has published numerous essays, reviews & poems in Gay journals throughout the country. His Gay experience is but one facet of a rich, complex and productive life. He currently teaches Victorian literature & poetry writing workshops at U. Cal. Irvine."

VINCENT SACARDI (died 1972)

Was a Boston Gay Liberationist. He had been a member of the Student Homophile League, the Gay Study Group, and Gay Male Liberation, and was on the staff of *Fag Rag*. He was also a writer who wrote constantly. But having come out didn't prevent him from taking his own life (October 11, 1972, in Boston). The poem printed in this anthology was found, undated, among his effects.

RON SCHREIBER (*Somerville, Mass.*)
"Was born in 1934 in Chicago & raised in Dayton, Ohio. He has lived—alone, with a lover, and, now, in a collective—in New York, Amsterdam, and Boston, where he works as a teacher. Two books of poetry: *Living Space* (Hanging Loose Press); and *Moving to a New Place* (Alice James Books); editor of one anthology of poems, *31 New American Poets* (New York, Hill & Wang, 1969)."

PERRY SCOTT
At the time his poem "Dicke" appeared in *Gay Sunshine* (February 1972), Perry Scott was living in New England. His present whereabouts are unknown.

CHARLEY SHIVELY (*Boston*)
"Sagittarius, born 8 Dec. 1937, Stonelick Township, Ohio. Sucked first cock at five; was fucked at twelve. Been with *Fag Rag* from the beginning with a poem in most every issue. I love to read aloud & try to tune myself with Jack Spicer, Frank O'Hara, Steve Jonas & John Wieners. My poems are oral and should be eaten raw. First book: *Nuestra Senora de los Dolores* (Boston Good Gay Poets, 1975)."

AARON SHURIN (*San Francisco*)
"Born 1947 in Manhattan, then to Texas, Beverly Hills and Berkeley, where my brother introduced me to Denise Levertov, whose great spirit helped waken in lazy me a storm of poetry. Left in 1969 for Cambridge and Cape Cod, where I lived with The Wasted Lives for Peace; learning from an amazing women's community how to be more nearly human; reorienting my life vision with brilliant ridiculous Gay Liberationists around Boston. Helped form the Good Gay Poets; writing, finally, as if there was something new to say. There was. I'm back in San Francisco now, making a home of it."

DAVID EMERSON SMITH (*Boston*)
"I never went to my senior prom/ while other boys were/ dick crocking their temples and juicy fruit gum on American Bandstand/ I was staring at the dandelions in my closet/ 1963/ my father died/ read poetry/ wrote poetry and preached poetry until it sprouted ears/ 1969/ 1971/ we taught each other how to listen and Claude Monet saw through the gray of the Thames./ Somewhere between Soho & So. Boston I taught my tears to sing/ oh yess/ one day I woke up gay/ not bad for a sea urchin from Narragansett Bay/ Born 1945/ now Good Gay Poet, Boston."

JACK SPICER (*1925-1965*)
Spicer lived most of his life in San Francisco and later in Vancouver, B.C. His books include: *After Lorca* (1957); *Billy the Kid* (1959); *The Heads of the Town up to the Aether* (1962); *Lament for the Makers* (1963); and *The Holy Grail* (1964). A collection of his books was published by Black Sparrow Press, 1975. *Manroot* No. 10 (Winter 1975) is a volume of poetry and prose tributes to Spicer.

GEORGE STANLEY (*Vancouver, B.C.*)
"Born in San Francisco, 1934; has published six books of poetry, the most recent are *You* (Vancouver: New Star Books, 1974) and *The Stick* (Vancouver: Talonbooks, 1975). He has been in the Army, has an M.A. in English (S.F. State, 1971) and has worked as a mail handler, warehouseman, clerk, librarian, accountant, journalist, publisher, and truck stripper."

RICHARD TAGETT (*Guerneville, Calif.*)

"Born in Ashtabula, 1936. A person, not always so easily assumed. Still fragmented, growing. Essentially self-educated—Japan, New York, San Francisco. With Paul Mariah co-editor of *Manroot* since its inception in 1969. Don't understand relationship of Humanity & Circumstance. Faith in The Instant—not these past details. Live with my friend, Jose Laffitte, near Russian River."

HUNCE VOELCKER (*Duncans Mills, Calif.*)

"Born on the banks of the Susquehanna River in Danville, Pennsylvania in 1940, and a little while later his first spoken word was cow. Then he was Eddie Barton's lover. Then he wrote *The Hart Crane Voyages*. Then he was Link's lover. Then he rewrote *Logan*. Then he wrote *Sillycomb*. Then he was everybody's lover. Then he wrote *Joy Rock Statue Ship*. Then he wrote *Songs for the Revolution*. Then he was Rodney Price's lover. Then he wrote *Parade of Gumdrop*. Then he finished writing *Sillycomb* when he was everybody's lover wishing that he was somebody's lover he built a house near Duncans Mills California and in it he is working on a book about *The Bridge*."

JOHN WIENERS (*Boston*)

Born in Boston in 1934, attended Black Mountain College under the tutorship of Charles Olson and Robert Duncan and co-founded the magazine *Measure*. His *Hotel Wentley Poems* (1958) brought him acclaim, and selections from his poetry appeared in Donald Allen's anthology *New American Poetry*. His other books of poetry include: *Ace of Pentacles; Pressed Wafer; Asylum Poems; Nerves; Selected Poems* (1972); and *Behind the State Capitol* or *Cincinnati Pike* (Good Gay Poets, Boston, 1975). See interview in *Gay Sunshine* No. 17 (March 1973).

JONATHAN WILLIAMS (*Dentdale, Yorkshire, England; and Highlands, N.C.*)

Describes himself as "poet, publisher, essayist, hiker, sorehead, and sybarite. He was born in Asheville, N.C. in 1929. Education: St. Albans School; uneducated: Princeton; re-educated: Atelier 17, The Institute of Design (Chicago) and Black Mountain College. Since 1951 he has been the director of The Jargon Society, a writer's press that publishes about four books a year devoted to new or ignored poets and photographers. Lives with Tom Meyer. They divide time between Corn Close, a stone cottage of 1650 in the Yorkshire Dales, and a house near Highlands, N.C. His major work at the moment is *364 Untinears & Antennae in Homage to Maurice Ravel*." Other books include: *An Ear in Bartram's Tree* and *The Loco Logodaedalist in Situ* (1972).

TERENCE WINCH (*Washington, D.C.*)

"I was born on All Saints Day 1945 in NYC and raised to think of myself as Irish as much as American by my parents who were off the boat. I started playing music when I was eight and writing poetry when I was sixteen which may mean something new is in store for me when I reach thirty-two." Recent books are: *Boning Up* (1972); and *Irish Musicians* (1974).

IAN YOUNG (*Toronto, Canada*)

"Was born in London in 1945, grew up in South Africa, Canada and England and has been active in the gay movement in Toronto since 1969. His books include: *White Garland, Cool Fire*, and *Lions in the Stream* (a trilogy written with Richard Phelan); *The Male Muse: A Gay Anthology; Year of the Quiet Sun; Double Exposure; Some Green Moths; Curieux d'Amour*; and a bibliography, *The Male Homosexual in Literature*. He is a contributing editor of *Gay Sunshine*. Current projects include a novel, a gay S&M anthology and a new Moth book."

Acknowledgments

The editor is especially grateful to the poets themselves for permission to publish their work. All poems copyrighted by the poets unless otherwise stated. Many of the poems in this anthology were originally published in magazines; some appeared in books by the individual poets; at least the first appearance in print is cited in each case. Abbreviations: *GS* = *Gay Sunshine* (San Francisco); *FR* = *Fag Rag* (Boston); *SQ* = *Sebastian Quill* (San Francisco); *MD* = *Mouth of the Dragon* (NYC).

HECTOR TITO ALVAREZ: "The Birth of the Political Angel"—*FR* 12, 1975. WILLIAM BARBER: All poems from *Abyss*, S.F., 1974 ("Gay Poet" appeared originally in *GS* 7, 1971, & "Hustler Joe" in *GS* 17, 1973; "A Fuck Poem" in *City* 5, 1969, & "Serial Poem" in *Manroot* 1, 1969). VICTOR BORSA: "Transvestia," "The Feel of Teeth," "Young Man Dancing"—*A Search for the Wild*, Fiddlehead Books, 1971; "I Speak with My Angel" & "The Sound"—*Manroot* 9, 1974. JOE BRAINARD: "I Remember" selections—*I Remember*, Full Court Press, 1975; "Pornographic Movie Plots"—all from *Z*, 1973. PERRY BRASS: "I Think the New Teacher's a Queer"—*GS* 18, 1973; "Fairy"—*GS* 14, 1972; "In Loving You"—*GS* 13, 1972. ADRIAN BROOKS: "Yes"—*GS* 24, 1975; "Circus"—*FR* 12, 1975. IRA COHEN: All poems from *GS* 24, 1975. KIRBY CONGDON: "Jagganath" & "Suns"—*Black Sun*, Pilot Press, 1973; "Horse Opera" & "Motorcyclist"—*Juggernaut*, Interim Books, 1966. ED COX: "Waking"—*GS* 24, 1975; "Waiting"—*Blocks*, Some Of Us Press, 1973; "Cruising"—*GS* 21, 1974; "Poem for Hart Crane" & "Windows"—*GPU News* vol. 4, no. 6, 1975. TIM DLUGOS: "Night Life"—*Painted Bride Quarterly* vol. 1, no. 3, 1974; "Famous Writers"—*Mass Transit* 3, 1974; "Day Light"—*GS* 23, 1974. ROBERT DUNCAN: See copyright page. DAVID EBERLY: "Dark of the Moon Nothing" & "Poem"—*FR* 3, 1972; "The Delsarte Method"—*FR* 12, 1975; "Short Letter"—*FR* 5, 1973. JIM EGGELING: "Thirteen . . ."—*FR* 10, 1974; "Chan Ex"—*GS* 14, 1972; "Invocation"—*GS* 24, 1975. KENWARD ELMSLIE: "Communique for Orpheus"—*Circus Nerves*, Black Sparrow Press, 1971. DANIEL EVANS: "Letter to Walt Whitman" —*GS* 23, 1974; "Eye Praise"—*GS* 21, 1974. GERALD FABIAN: "Elegy for a Lost Shipmate"—*Odissea Finita*, Very Stone House Press, 1969. SALVATORE FARINELLA: "Tonight"—*Manroot* 6/7, 1972; "Epithalamion"—*FR* 10, 1974; "I Haven't Heard . . ."—*SQ* 3, 1972; "New Each Time" & "Winter Kill"—*SQ* 2, 1971; "Dead End Orgy"—*GS* 17, 1973; "The Experience"—*GS* 18, 1973; "July 4th Threesome"—*MD* 3, 1974. EDWARD FIELD: "The Moving Man"—*The Male Muse*, Crossing Press, 1973; "Street Instructions: At the Crotch"—*GS* 24, 1975. CHARLES HENRI FORD: "Their Images I Loved I View in Thee" & "Candy Darling"—*GS* 24, 1975. JAMES GIANCARLO: "Angels of Light"—*Manroot* 9, 1974. ALLEN GINSBERG: See copyright page; "Night Gleam"—*GS* 22/*FR* 9, 1974. JOHN GIORNO: "I sat on his face . . ."—*GS* 22/*FR* 9, 1974; "Pornographic Poem"—*Poems by John Giorno*, Mother Press, 1967; "I reached . . ."—*Cancer in My Left Ball*, Something Else Press, 1973. ROBERT GLUCK: "Meditation: Ed"—*GS* 23, 1974; "Poem"—*Panjandrum* 2/3, 1973. PAUL GOODMAN: See copyright page. STEVE JONAS: "An Ode for Garcia Lorca"—*Transmutations*, Ferry Press, 1966; "Discourse," "On the Esplanade," "Poem," & "Blackstone Park"—*Caterpillar* 15/16, 1971. E. A. LACEY: All poems from *Path of Snow: Poems 1951-1973*, Ahasuerus Press, 1974. MICHAEL LALLY: "Their Imagination Safe"

—*New* 24, 1974. GERRIT LANSING: "Amazing Grace and a Salad Bowl"—*Caterpillar* 18, 1972; "Boxcar Moonlight Scene," "Alba," & "3 from Cock Haiku"—*FR* 4, 1973; "A Ghazel of Absence"—*Signal*, Fall 1963. WINSTON LEYLAND: "Angel Metamorphosis" I—*GS* 4, 1970; II—*GS* 10, 1971. GERARD MALANGA: "Numbers"—*GS* 20, 1973. PAUL MARIAH: "Quarry Rock"—*Personae Non Gratae*, Shameless Hussy Press, 1971; "Imaginary Letter of Young Caesar . . ."—*Six Imaginary Letters of Young Caesar on the Bythenian Tour, 81 B.C.*, Manroot Books, 1974; "The Spoon Ring"—*The Spoon Ring*, Contraband Press, 1973, & Manroot Books, 1974; "Textures"—*MD* 2, 1974; "The Figa"—*GS* 2, 1970. WAYNE McNEILL: "I Wonder If Verlaine Held Rimbaud"—*GS* 21, 1974. TAYLOR MEAD: "Autobiography"—*Excerpts from the Anonymous Diary of a New York Youth*, N.Y., 1961; "Incredible crotch-burning child light . . ." & "Young grooving . . ."—*On Amphetamine and in Europe*, Boss Books, 1968; "I wrote this poem . . ."—*Ant's Forefoot* 7; diary excerpts—*Anonymous Diary of a New York Youth*, vol. 1, 1961; vol. 2, 1962; vol. 3 (*On Amphetamine and in Europe*), 1968. THOMAS MEYER: "Boy Muse, Uranian Roses for Strato"—*GS* 22/*FR* 9, 1974. JAMES MITCHELL: "How to Become a Hero of Homosexuality"—*SQ* 1, 1970; "Jesse, I blew it at the baths!" & "The Orgy"—*SQ* 2, 1971; "I Want to Sleep with Toshiro Mifune"—*Manroot* 5, 1971. JAMES NOLAN: "Jilala"—*GS* 17, 1973. HAROLD NORSE: See copyright page; "Let Me Love You All at Stillman's Gym"—*GS* 22/*FR* 9, 1973; "Green Ballet"—*GS* 10, 1972; the three Mohammed poems originally appeared in *GS* 18, 1973. FRANK O'HARA: See copyright page. CHUCK ORTLEB: "The Hustler" & "Some Boys"—*GS* 24, 1975. STAN PERSKY: "Slaves" & "Swans"—*Slaves*, New Star Books, 1974. ROBERT PETERS: All poems from *Cool Zebras of Light*, Christopher's Books, 1974 ("A Celebration" & "On Being Ravished by an Angel" originally appeared in *GS* 8, 1971; "Love as Pusher" & "On Pushing a Lover" in *GS* 21, 1974). VINCENT SACARDI: "Ode to a Suicide"—*FR* 5, 1973. RON SCHREIBER: "Phantasies & Facts"—*GS* 23, 1974; "The Image of You Vivid"—*New;* "Kaosan's Robe"—*GS* 22/*FR* 9, 1974; "1/3"—*GS* 17, 1973. PERRY SCOTT: "Dicke"—*GS* 11, 1972. CHARLEY SHIVELY: "Carrots Farewell"—*Stone Soup Poetry* 15, 1974; "Continental Drift"—*FR* 5, 1973; "For Steve Jonas"—*FR* 10, 1974; "Immediately"—*GS* 18, 1973; "Snow Poem"—*Liberation: SHL News* (Boston), 1970. AARON SHURIN: "Exorcism of the Straight/Man/Demon"—*GS* 17, 1973. D. E. SMITH: "L Street Elite" & "L Street Expose" from "L Street"—*FR* 12, 1975. JACK SPICER: All poems copyright for the Spicer Estate by Robin Blaser. Reprinted with permission of Stan Persky. "A Prayer for Pvt. Graham Mackintosh on Halloween," "Five Words for Joe Dunn," "Orpheus' Song to Apollo," & "We find the body difficult to speak"—*Caterpillar* 12, 1970; "Some Notes on Whitman"—*Manroot* 6/7, 1972; "Central Park West"—*Measure* 3, 1962, & *Manroot* 10, 1975; "Chapter IV: Rimbaud"—*The Heads of the Town up to the Aether*, Auerhahn Press, 1962; "For you I would build . . ."—*Language*, White Rabbit Press, 1965. GEORGE STANLEY: "Touching"—*You*, New Star Books, 1974. RICHARD TAGETT: "Dear Alfred Charles Kinsey"—*Empty Elevator Shaft* 1, 1974; "Want"—*SQ* 2, 1971; "Way II"—*GS* 23, 1974; "With Head Laying on Soft Cock"—*Manroot* 4, 1971. HUNCE VOELCKER: "Earth, Pt. 1" & "Great Spirit, Pt. 2"—*Songs for the Revolution*, Cowstone Press, 1969. JOHN WIENERS: "A Poem for the Old Man"—*Hotel Wentley Poems*, Auerhahn Press, © 1958 by John Wieners; "Impasse" & "The Old Man"—*Pressed Wafer*, Gallery Upstairs Press, 1967; "Act 2" & "Two Years Later"—*Ace of Pentacles*, J. F. Carr & Robert Wilson, N.Y., © 1972 John Wieners; "How to Cope with This"—*Nerves*, Cape Goliard Press, © 1970 John Wieners ("A Poem for the Old Man," "Impasse," "The Old Man," "Act 2," & "In Love" also appeared in *Selected Poems*, Grossman Pub., © 1972 by John Wieners); "Ballade"—*The Magazine for Further Studies*, Buffalo, & *Manroot* 10, 1975; "Contemplation"—*GS* 17, 1973; "Gusta with Madame Simone de Beauvoir" —*GS* 22/*FR* 9, 1974; all poems reprinted with permission of John Wieners. JONATHAN WILLIAMS: "Lexington Nocturne" & "Modern Love Lyric"—*Adventures with a Twelve-Inch Pianist Beyond the Blue Horizon,* Xerox Edit., N.M., copyright © 1973 by Jonathan Williams ("Lexington Nocturne" also published in *GS* 22/*FR* 9, 1974); "How Do You Get It All Out" & "The Apocryphal Oracular Yeah-Sayings of the Ersatz Mae West"—*The Loco Logodaedalist in Situ,* Cape Goliard Press/Grossman Pub., 1972, copyright © 1971 by Jonathan Williams; "The Honey Lamb"—*An Ear in Bartram's Tree,* Univ. of N. Carolina Press, 1969, & New Directions, 1972, copyright © 1962, 1969 by Jonathan Williams. All poems reprinted with permission of Jonathan Williams. TERENCE WINCH: "The Jungle"—*Everybody's Ex-Lover,* Washington, D.C. IAN YOUNG: "Sky/Eyes"—*Writ* 1, 1970; "Angel"—*GS* 9, 1971, & *The Male Muse,* Crossing Press, 1973; "Colossus of Rhodes"—*GS* 9, 1971, & *Some Green Moths,* Catalyst Press, 1972; "A Sugar Candy Bird"—*Double Exposure,* Crossing Press, 1970; "The Skull"—*Year of the Quiet Sun,* House of Anansi, 1969; "Two Moths for Richard" & "Chinese Boy, 14"—*GS* 23, 1974; "Japanese Boy" & "Epping"—*Some Green Moths,* Catalyst Press, 1972.

Graphics: EDWARD AULERICH from *Andy* by Robert Gluck, Panjandrum Press, 1973. JOE BRAINARD from *GS* 23, 1974. CZANARA: "Hermaphrodite-Angel of Peladan" from *The Other Face of Love* by Raymond de Becker, Bell Pub., N.Y. 1969. SAMUEL REESE: prison lino cut from *GS* 20, 1974. BRUCE REIFEL: "Gay Brothers & Sisters Unite!" from *GS* 8, 1971. WILTON DAVID (gleep) from *GS* 22/*FR* 9, 1974.

Manufactured in the United States of America